A QUICK REFERENCE GUIDE FOR AN

MOBILE OFFENSIVE SECURITY POCKET GUIDE

A QUICK REFERENCE GUIDE FOR ANDROID AND IOS

MOBILE OFFENSIVE SECURITY POCKET GUIDE

JAMES STEVENSON

MOBILE OFFENSIVE SECURITY POCKET GUIDE -
A QUICK REFERENCE GUIDE FOR ANDROID AND IOS

James Stevenson
UK

ISBN-13 (pbk): 978-1-3999-2195-4
ISBN-13 (electronic): 978-1-3999-2196-1

Author: James Stevenson | www.jamesstevenson.me
Editor: Nic Carter | www.fiverr.com/thisisstrange
Formatting: Formatted Books | www.formattedbooks.com

For information on translations, reprint, paperback, or audio rights, please communicate with the author directly, at www.jamesstevenson.me.

CONTENTS

ABOUT THE AUTHOR

 James Stevenson has been working in the programming and computer security industry for over 5 years. Most of that has been working as an Android software engineer and vulnerability researcher. Before this, James graduated with a BSc in computer security in 2017. James has previously published the book Android Software Internals Quick Reference, with Apress publishing in 2021.

At the time of writing, James is a full-time security researcher, part-time Ph.D. student, and occasional conference speaker. Outside of Android internals, James' research has also focused on offender profiling and cybercrime detection capabilities.

For more information and contact details, visit https://JamesStevenson.me.

CHAPTER ONE

INTRODUCTION

Mobile Offensive Security comes in many flavors—from application security and operating system internals to the vulnerability research of the baseband and other processors. This book attempts to summarize all of these unique areas of mobile offensive security into a handy and easy-to-use pocket guide.

While this pocket guide is not exhaustive in all things mobile offensive security, it sets the groundwork for how and where you can go to further your knowledge in specific areas.

Towards the end of this book, you will also find a series of challenges that summarize the key areas of many of the book's chapters if you are looking to put your knowledge to the test.

What This Book Is

- An introduction to the concepts of Reverse Engineering, Mobile Offensive Security, and other Mobile Security systems such as Baseband.
- An easy-to-digest pocket guide detailing fundamental knowledge, principles, and methods related to mobile offensive security.
- A reference guide for reverse engineering principles and approaches.
- A guide for offensive security engagements, including Frida and dynamic instrumentation references.
- An introduction to baseband and a methodology to follow when it comes to reverse engineering baseband implementations.
- A summary guide for iOS and Android architectures and security assessment methodologies.
- A collection of challenges, useful for putting the knowledge to the test.

What This Book Is Not

- A list of zero-days or exploits for mobile devices or modern baseband implementations.
- A completely exhaustive list of exploits, approaches, or techniques—this is a pocket guide.

Tools Used Throughout The Book

- IDA Pro – https://hex-rays.com/ida-pro/
- Ghidra – https://ghidra-sre.org/
- GDB – https://www.gnu.org/software/gdb/
- Jadx – https://github.com/skylot/jadx
- APK Tool – https://ibotpeaches.github.io/Apktool/
- Frida – https://frida.re/
- Frida iOS Dump – https://github.com/AloneMonkey/frida-ios-dump
- FriDump – https://github.com/Nightbringer21/fridump
- Objection – https://github.com/sensepost/objection

- Android Debug Bridge (ADB) – https://developer.android.com/studio/command-line/adb
- dex2jar – https://sourceforge.net/projects/dex2jar/
- JD GUI – http://java-decompiler.github.io/
- AFL++ – https://github.com/AFLplusplus/AFLplusplus
- Checkra1n – https://checkra.in/
- Quark – https://github.com/quark-engine/quark-engine
- Drozer – https://labs.f-secure.com/tools/drozer/

CHAPTER TWO

REVERSE ENGINEERING FUNDAMENTALS

The first chapter of this book goes through fundamental reverse engineering principles and techniques used throughout this book. For the purpose of this book, we will be using the Merriam Webster definition of reverse engineering in the context of product and application security, this being:

> *To disassemble and examine or analyse in detail [a product or device] to discover the concepts involved in manufacture, usually to produce something similar.*

What This Section Is

- An introduction to reverse engineering concepts, methodologies, and approaches.

- An introduction to vulnerability research practical starting points.
- An introduction to assembly and the ARM instruction set.

What This Section Is Not

- An overbearing step by step guide for reverse engineering a system.

Tools Used Throughout This Section

- IDA Pro – https://hex-rays.com/ida-pro/
- Ghidra – https://ghidra-sre.org/
- GDB – https://www.gnu.org/software/gdb/
- Frida – https://frida.re/
- Jadx – https://github.com/skylot/jadx
- APK Tool – https://ibotpeaches.github.io/Apktool/

Reverse Engineering in UK Law

A question that comes up a lot when it comes to reverse engineering and one that should be addressed sooner rather than later is if reverse engineering is legal. In UK copyright law:

- There is no provision for decompilation and no fair use defense if the reverse engineering is for commercial research or study.
- There is also no fair use for copying during decompilation.
- However, reverse engineering for interoperability purposes is allowed.

So in actuality, the law isn't especially clear. However, in practice, the answer is yes, to a degree, if you own the program locally. Just be smart about it, and try not to breach any T&Cs. However, please note that I am not a lawyer; this is my opinion and not legal advice.

Research Theory

Research methodologies and research theory can be applied to an array of research projects. As reverse engineering requires a research mindset, it is important to apply such a research theory. Figure 1 - Research Theory Flow Diagram shows a method for approaching reverse engineering (and other research) problems. Here examples are given for a static code review. However, this method applies to all reverse engineering and research approaches.

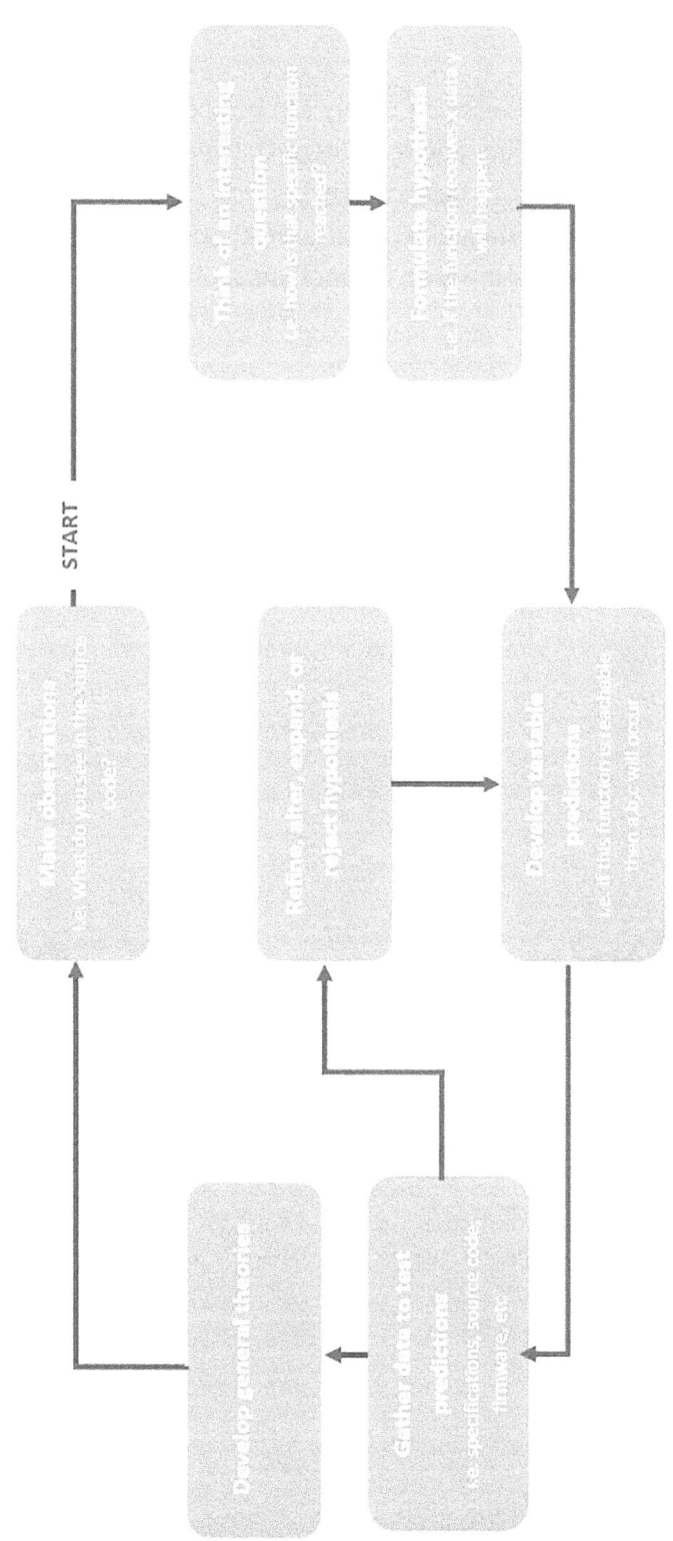

Figure 1 - Research Theory Flow Diagram

The Reverse Engineering and Product Security Umbrella

There are many places to start regarding reverse engineering, many types of products to review, and a myriad of different approaches that fall into the reverse engineering or product security review umbrella. Some of these are listed in Table 1- Reverse engineering and product security umbrella.

Category	Actions
Documentation Review	When reviewing published software or hardware, a common initial phase is to identify and review available documentation—this could include high-level design documentation, how-to guides, architecture diagrams, source code, and more.
Attack Surface Mapping	Another initial phase of reverse engineering and vulnerability research is to identify the attack surface of the software or product being reviewed. This involves identifying all communication vectors and interfaces for the system and how a threat actor could utilise them to gain access to the system.
Hardware Analysis	During this phase (only applicable to physical devices), it's important to identify and assess all physical interfaces (i.e., JTAG, RS232, etc.). During this phase, it is also pertinent to identify any tamper detection mechanisms in place and to identify their effectiveness. It may also be pertinent to extract the firmware from the target device.
Reverse Engineering	This phase involves taking any black-box software components or firmware that you have access to and identifying key components (commonly via disassembling them). This phase may also involve emulating key software components to understand programme flow.
Communication Security	As part of the attack surface phase, the communication interfaces used by the device or software should have been mapped. During this phase, it's important to examine any security mechanisms in place on top of those communication channels—including encryption and certificate pinning.

Fuzzing	As part of an in-depth review of a system, it may be pertinent to develop or use a fuzzer to trigger complex bugs in the system. Fuzzer's use unexpected and random data provided as input with the goal of attempting to cause a crash and identify a vulnerability.
Vulnerability Identification	Depending on the type of research being performed, it may be pertinent to review the system for potential vulnerabilities. If this is the case, outcomes of the above phases can be used to identify vulnerabilities in the system.
Remediation Identification	Once a vulnerability has been identified, it is critical to focus on it and identify how the vulnerability can be remediated and fixed.

Table 1- Reverse engineering and product security umbrella

Practical Starting Points

The below lists a summary of practical starting points that can be applied to any reverse engineering engagement:

- Review the products **specifications** for entry points (e.g., where a message/data is received).
- Identify large or **complex functions** in the source code.
- Look at **libraries and imports.**
- If on an operating system (OS) with a strong sandboxing, look at what **permissions** are available.
- Use **strings** and log statements to identify functionality.
- Look at **function and variable names** if not obfuscated.
- Look at how **comms** (i.e. network traffic) are performed and if data can be intercepted.
- If running on proprietary hardware, look at approaches for **emulation.**

FUNDAMENTAL CONCEPTS

Static VS. Dynamic Analysis

Static Analysis – Examining source, decompiled, or disassembled code in an attempt to understand the flow of an application (including entry points, permissions, communications, and potentially vulnerable functions).

Dynamic Analysis – The analysis of a program by running on a real or virtual processor. Commonly associated with black-box testing, debuggers, or fuzzing approaches.

File Formats

- **PE** – Portable Executable. Common on Windows.
- **ELF** – Executable and Linkable Format. Common on Android and Linux.
- **APK** – Android Package. The file format used for Android applications. Once unbundled, an APK will include one or several class files; these contain the actual assembled code.
- **Mach-O** – Mach object file format – MacOS and iOS. An iOS application will take the form of an IPA file. However, once unbundled will take the form of a Mach-O file, of which contains the actual assembled code.
- **Other formats** – Countless formats are common when reverse engineering. Most modern disassemblers such as IDA and Ghidra will be able to identify these formats when presented with a binary. Some additional formats include: EXE, Binary, MS-DOS, DEX, XBOX Executable, JAR, ZIP archive, etc.

Disassembling & Decompiling

Decompiling – A decompiler will take an assembled file and attempt to create a high-level source file (e.g., C, Java, etc.). This source file represents the decompiler's best guess at what the original source would have looked like and is commonly referred to as pseudo-code.

Disassembling – A disassembler takes machine code (i.e., a binary file) and translates that into assembly language (i.e., x86 or ARM assembly).

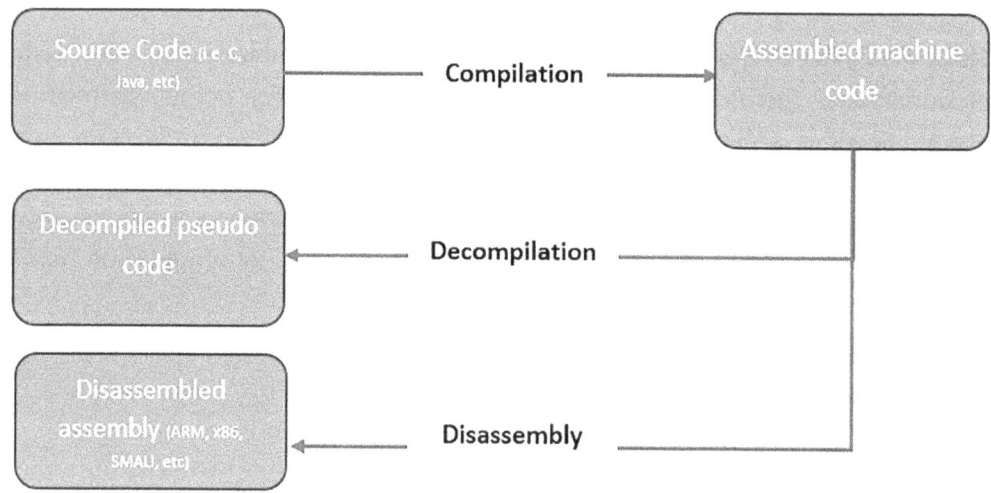

Figure 2 - Disassembly and decompilation diagram

Threads and Processes

At a high level, a process relates to an instance of an executing program, where one or more threads can run in the context of a process. A process can be Running (Active), Sleeping (Inactive), or Zombie (completed, with an entry remaining in the process table). A thread is a unit in which the operating system allocates processor time. A Windows service and Linux daemon are non-interactive processes that run in the background.

Patching

Patching is the process of modifying an already existing file (PE, binary, DEX, etc.). Due to the nature of disassembling, patching is commonly done on disassembled code, as this can then be reassembled. Use cases for patching include subverting a security mechanism, adding additional functionality, or reaching previously unused code. More information can be found on patching in the section Patching an APK on page 33.

Hooking

Hooking is the process of intercepting function calls, messages, and events passed between software components. Examples include: hooking the function call isPasswordSecure() to always return True, intercepting mouse and keyboard events, and intercepting operating system calls. More information can be found on hooking and specifically dynamic instrumentation in the section What Is Instrumentation on page 40.

Stack and Heap

Understanding the stack and heap is critical when performing low-level reverse engineering and vulnerability research. Information on these data structures can be seen in Table 2 - Stack versus heap.

Stack	Heap
The stack is a linear structure in memory where information is stored sequentially in blocks.	The Heap is a region of memory used for dynamic allocation. With this approach, the data is stored randomly.
Memory in the Stack is allocated automatically for variables, and the scope of which is local to each block.	Memory in the Heap is managed explicitly, and the variables are created or initialized at runtime.
The stack is used for static memory allocation. This means that memory is allocated at compile time before a program's execution.	Unlike the Stack, the Heap is used for dynamic memory allocating. This means that memory in the Heap can be allocated and freed in an arbitrary and non-consecutive order.

When a new function is called, a new block is pushed onto the stack with its own set of local variables. This block is, in turn, popped off the stack when the function returns.

Memory on the Heap provides a wider surface for memory leaks and corruption attacks. One reason for this is that memory can be allocated to unused objects.

One of the main advantages of the Stack is that access to memory is fast as items in a stack are arranged in a last-in, first-out order.

Compared to the Stack, access to memory in a heap is slower due to it being managed manually.

Table 2 - Stack versus heap

Stack and Heap C example

Below is an example where a char array size 255 is created on the stack and on the heap. As discussed above, the main difference here is at what stage the program knows to allocate the memory for the variables—where on the stack, this is defined at compilation, and for the heap, it is declared at run time.

The below shows how a variable can be defined in Stack memory:

```
char buffer[255];
```

The below example shows a pointer to the buffer (as pBuffer) defined on the stack and the data at that pointer, new char[255], defined on the heap.

```
char *pBuffer;
pBuffer = new char[255];
delete[] pBuffer;
```

Assembly

Assembly language (often referred to as asm) is any low-level programming language (ARM, x86, Dalvik, etc.) where there is a strong relationship between the language and the architecture's machine code. Because assembly has this tight relationship with the architecture, every assembly language is designed for exactly one specific computer architecture.

The process of converting source code to an executable is referred to as compilation. The process of converting human-readable assembly instructions to an executable is called assembly. The terms decompile and disassemble are used for the reverse.

Assembly often supports comments, macros, and symbolic labels. However, outside of this, it commonly has one statement per instruction.

ARM

For the purpose of this explanation, this chapter will focus on the ARM assembly language. ARM is used in Android, iOS, a small handful of Windows devices, and modern macOS devices.

This section will cover the core principles and techniques required for working with assembly and serve as a building block when needing to use other assembly languages (such as x86).

Instructions

Assembly languages use mnemonics to represent each low-level machine instruction or opcode. These mnemonics are human-readable, and In ARM, most mnemonics take the form of three-letter words (i.e., SUB, MOV, STR, etc.). Additional letters (called optional suffixes) can be added to the mnemonic to give it further meaning and utility—for example, adding L to B (branch) to make BL (branch with a link).

Following a mnemonic will be a series of conditions, registers, or operands. An example structure of this is: `<mnemonic>{optional suffic}{condition} {register}, operand1, operand2`.

Data Types

Signed data types can hold both positive and negative values, and are therefore lower in range.

Unsigned data types can hold large positive values (including 'Zero') but cannot hold negative values and are therefore wider in range.

For example, a byte has a total of 256 combinations. An unsigned byte's values can be between 0 and 255, while a signed (i.e., the value being preceded with +/-) byte's values can be between -128 to 127 (one bit is lost for representing the sign).

In addition to this, there are several categories of data length: byte, half-word, and word. A visual example of this is shown in Figure 3 - Word, Half Word, and Byte example.

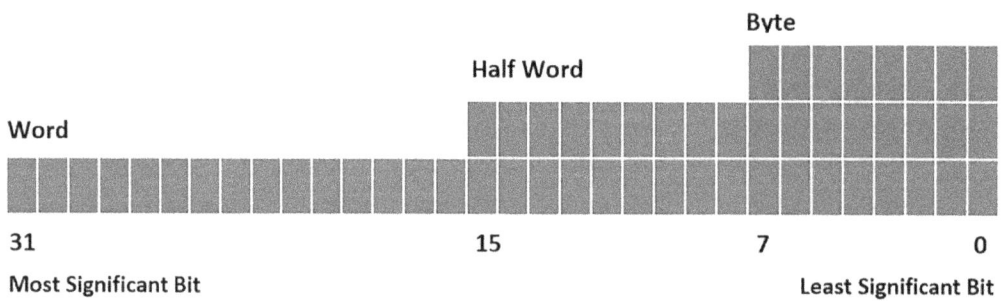

Figure 3 - Word, Half Word, and Byte example

Endianness

Endianness is used to view bytes in memory and define the byte order.

- **Little-endian** – the least-significant-byte is stored at the lowest address (the address closest to zero).
- **Big-endian** – the most-significant-byte is stored at the lowest address

ARM version 3+ is bi-endian, which means that it features a setting that allows for switchable endianness. A visual example of endianness is shown in Figure 4 - Endianness Explained.

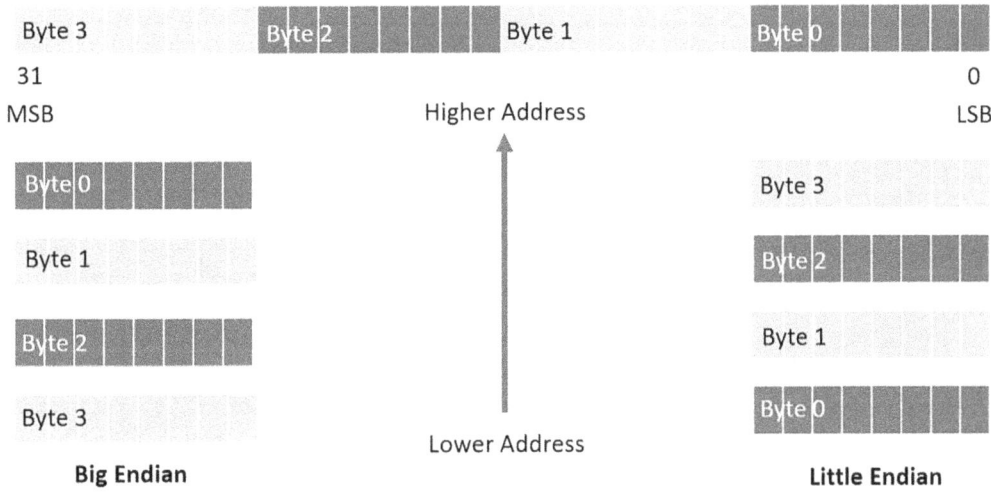

Figure 4 - Endianness Explained

Registers

Registers are locations within the processor and are used to store data. Unlike Random-access memory (RAM), access to registers is effectively instantaneous (Where reads from main memory can take hundreds of CPU cycles to return).

Another way of phrasing this would be that registers are small amounts of fast-access memory integrated into the CPU.

While some registers are reserved for special purposes, all registers can hold any value, including addresses (pointers), results from mathematical operations, characters, etc. A list of registers can be seen in Table 3 - ARM Registers.

#	Alias	Purpose
R0	–	General purpose
R1	–	General purpose
R2	–	General purpose
R3	–	General purpose
R4	–	General purpose
R5	–	General purpose
R6	–	General purpose
R7	–	Holds Syscall Number
R8	–	General purpose
R9	–	General purpose
R10	–	General purpose
R11	FP	Frame Pointer
Special Purpose Registers		
R12	IP	Intra Procedural Call
R13	SP	Stack Pointer
R14	LR	Link Register
R15	PC	Program Counter
CPSR	–	Current Program Status Register

Table 3 - ARM Registers

Instructions

A subsection of the most common ARM instructions can be seen in Table 4 - Example ARM Instructions.

Instruction	Description
MOV	Move data
MVN	Move and negate
ADD	Addition
SUB	Subtraction
MUL	Multiplication
LSL	Logical Shift Left
LSR	Logical Shift Right
ASR	Arithmetic Shift Right
ROR	Rotate Right
CMP	Compare
AND	Bitwise AND
ORR	Bitwise OR
EOR	Bitwise XOR
LDR	Load
STR	Store
LDM	Load Multiple
STM	Store Multiple
PUSH	Push on Stack
POP	Pop off Stack
B	Branch
BL	Branch with Link
BX	Branch and eXchange
BLX	Branch with Link and eXchange
SWI/SVC	System Call

Table 4 - Example ARM Instructions

For a full list of the ARM instruction set: https://iitd-plos.github.io/col718/ref/arm-instructionset.pdf

Tooling Synopsys

Specific tools will be discussed in their respective sections, and download links are provided at the start of each chapter where a tool is used. This section provides a general synopsis of some of the most common tools used in the reverse engineering field and those used for iOS and Android reverse engineering.

IDA (Interactive Disassembler)

- IDA Pro is the premium version of IDA and contains the full functionality, barring the hex-rays decompiler, an optional ad-on.
- Released in 2005
- Significant changes between IDA 6.x-7.3 and 7.4
- A separate version for 32 and 64 bit
- Optional paid Hex-Rays Decompiler IDA extension

Ghidra

- Ghidra is a free and open-source alternative to IDA Pro.
- Developed and released by the US National Security Agency (NSA) in March 2019
- Free built-in decompiler view.

GDB (GNU Debugger)

- Allows for the tracing and altering of the execution of a program. Modifying registers, flow, etc
- Supports: Ada, Assembly, C, C++, D, Fortran, Go, Objective-C, OpenCL, Modula-2, Pascal, and Rust
- The effectiveness of debugging will depend on if debugging/ symbol information was retained in the executable. To do this, use the gcc –g flag.
- GDB attach command to debug a running process

Frida

- A dynamic code instrumentation toolkit
- Inject snippets of JavaScript or your own library into native apps on Windows, macOS, GNU/Linux, iOS, Android, and QNX.
- Python API and JavaScript debugging
- The JavaScript is injected into the target processes—where it gets executed with full access to memory. This, in turn, allows for hooking functions inside the process.

JADX:

- Decompiles Dalvik bytecode to java classes from APK, dex, aar, and zip files
- Decodes AndroidManifest.xml and other resources from `resources.arsc`
- Simple IDE features like full-text search, find usage, and jump to declaration
- Projects can be exported to an Android Gradle project
- UI and command-line tool

APKTool:

- Disassembly of dex files to Smali (a human-readable representation of the Dalvik machine code)
- Can decode application resources
- Can be used to rebuild an APK after modification (patching)
- Command-line tool

CHAPTER THREE

MOBILE APPLICATION REVERSE ENGINEERING

A critical aspect of offensive mobile security is the ability to reverse engineer and identify issues in mobile applications. Many see this as the bread and butter of mobile offensive security, where the techniques discussed in the Reverse Engineering chapter can be applied to mobile applications.

What This Section Is

- A reference guide for common techniques required when performing mobile security reviews.
- A summary of key aspects of mobile applications and their purpose in security reviews.

What This Section Is Not

- An exhaustive list of mobile security approaches and methods.
- A list of zero-days.

Tools Used Throughout This Section

- Android Debug Bridge (ADB) – https://developer.android.com/studio/command-line/adb
- Ghidra – https://ghidra-sre.org/
- IDA Pro – https://hex-rays.com/ida-pro/
- dex2jar – https://sourceforge.net/projects/dex2jar/
- Jadx-gui – https://github.com/skylot/jadx
- APK Tool – https://ibotpeaches.github.io/Apktool/
- JD GUI – http://java-decompiler.github.io/
- Frida iOS Dump – https://github.com/AloneMonkey/frida-ios-dump
- Checkra1n – https://checkra.in
- Quark – https://github.com/quark-engine/quark-engine
- Drozer – https://labs.f-secure.com/tools/drozer/

Privileged Control of a Device (Rooting and Jailbreaking)

Both Android and iOS have a concept of privileged control on a device. Here, when talking about privileged control, it refers to providing a user with extensive controls over the device, which the manufacturer did not intend for the end-user to have and can normally allow for actions such as breaking application sandboxing, accessing and modifying system actions, and accessing the underlying kernel. For Android and iOS accessing such privileged control is referred to as rooting and jailbreaking respectfully.

Many of the actions discussed in this chapter and book may require the end-user of the device to have root or jailbroken access to a device. This section discusses the broad strokes for how this can be attained.

There are two broad categories of accessing privileged control of a device. These are:

- **Privileged control through manufacturer** – This is where the manufacturer of the device and operating system have put measures in place to allow the end-user to achieve a privileged state. This is common on some Android devices (i.e., the Google Pixel range), where it is possible to unlock the bootloader of a device, and then a new firmware/ system image can be written directly to the device.
- **Privileged control through vulnerability** – Varying from device to device and vulnerability to vulnerability. This is where a vulnerability is found in the underlying firmware or operating system that allows for control of the underlying system. Once used and control of the device gained, a custom firmware image can be flashed to the device.

Android

It's common to see both privileged control through manufacturer and privileged control through vulnerability when it comes to Android devices. Due to the variety of devices, it would be impossible to cover the process for rooting every Android device here. Instead, this section will cover the broad strokes required to root an Android device (specifically a Google Pixel device[1]):

1. Unlock the bootloader
   - Acquire Developer Options on your device (`System -> About phone -> tap Build number` until the prompt confirms developer options are enabled).
   - Enter developer options and enable OEM unlocking (`System -> Developer options -> OEM unlocking`)
   - Boot the device into the fastboot interface with `Power + volume down` when the device is off or starting up as normal.
   - Plug the device into a PC with Android Platform-tools installed (available from Android Studio) and run `fastboot flashing unlock`.
2. Patch the stock boot image using Magisk Manager

---

[1] https://source.android.com/setup/build/running#booting-into-fastboot-mode

- ▫ Identify and download the firmware image for your device version (https://developers.google.com/android/images).
- ▫ Extract the `boot.img` file from the archive and copy it to the device.
- ▫ Install the latest Magisk manager APK onto the device. This can be acquired from the GitHub repository (https://github.com/topjohnwu/Magisk/releases).
- ▫ Open the Magisk manager application and install the `boot.img` file. Select `Install` -> `Patch File` -> the `boot.img` file.

3. Flash the patched boot image
   - ▫ The previous step will generate a `magisk_patched.img` file, copy this onto the PC and once again reboot the device into fastboot mode (as performed above).
   - ▫ On the PC, run `fastboot flash boot magisk_patched.img`

iOS

Privileged control through the manufacturer is not common on iOS devices, and instead, most jailbreaks are performed via privileged control through vulnerability.

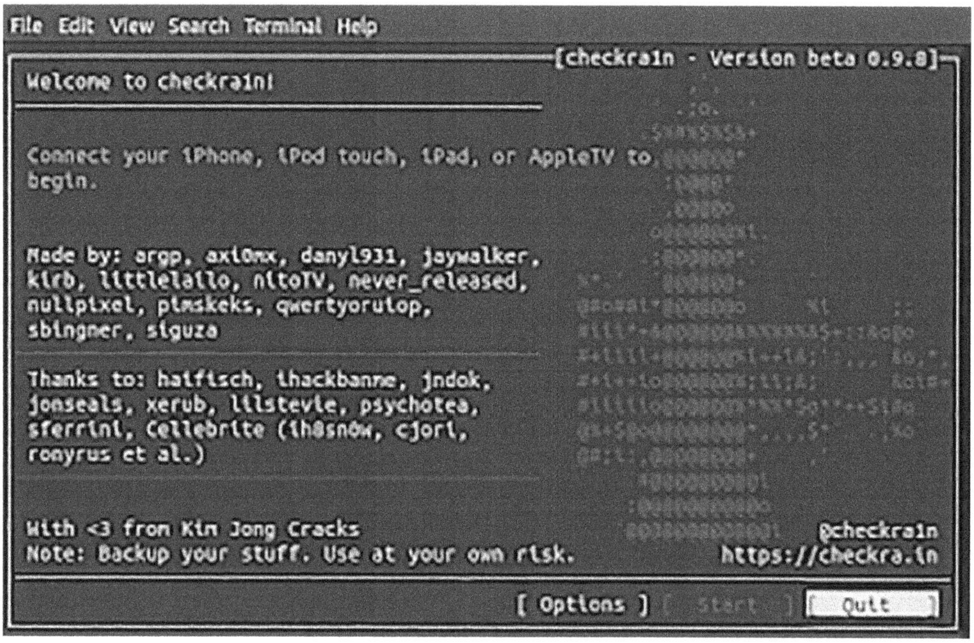

Figure 5 - Checkra1n UI

One such example of privileged control through vulnerability for iOS devices is checkra1n. Checkra1n supports 64-bit A5-A11 devices running iOS 12.0 or later from the iPhone 5s to the iPhone X (with the exception of a handful of devices, including the: iPad Air 2, iPad 5th generation, and iPad Pro 1st generation). Checkra1n is based on a BootROM exploit called checkm8. The Checkra1n jailbreak does not persist over reboot, which means that the device will need to be exploited once again if restarted.

- Once Checkra1n is downloaded onto a compatible Linux or MacOS PC and a compatible iOS device is connected, the checkra1n binary can be run (i.e., `./checkra1n`).
- Depending on your device model, you may need to enable the `Allow untested iOS/ PadOS/ tvOS versions` option.
- Select Start and follow the on-screen instructions.

Application Fundamentals

In both iOS and Android, the application is an archive of multiple files. On Android, this file is referred to as an APK, and on iOS an IPA file. These archives can be renamed to a zip file, decompressed, and have their contents extracted. In some cases, this is not the best approach for reverse-engineering the files, so custom tools exist for proper extraction (i.e., for Android APK tool and Jadx-gui can be used, while Ghidra can be used for reviewing iOS MacO files).

Inside these archives contains the actual file that is to be run. As Android uses the Java runtime, these files are `classes.dex` files (compiled Dalvik assembly), while in iOS, it is a MacO binary.

iOS application architecture

- **Info.plist:** Containing application-specific configurations.
- **_CodeSignature**: If this file is present, it denotes that the application has been signed.
- **Assets.car:** A zipped archive containing application assets (i.e., icons, etc.).
- **Frameworks**: Containing the application native libraries as `.dylib` or `.framework` files.

- **PlugIns**: Used for storing application extensions and modules (stored as `.appex` files).
- **Core Data**: Used to store application data—including offline data, temporary cache data, and functionality such as undoing actions.
- **PkgInfo**: The `PkgInfo` provides an alternate way to specify the `type` and `creator` codes of an application or bundle.
- The **MachO** file is located inside the extracted IPA file inside the `<application-name>.app` folder.
- **en.lproj, fr.proj, Base.lproj, etc.**: The naming convention for language packs containing specific resources for their respective language. `Base.Iproj` is the base language pack if one isn't provided.

Android application architecture

- **assets** – A directory for application assets. This is for arbitrary storage; anything provided by the application creator can be stored here.
- **res** – A directory with all resources that are not compiled into `resources.arsc` (icons, images, etc.).
- **lib** – A directory for native libraries used by the application. Contains multiple directories for each supported CPU architecture that the application has been compiled for.
- **META-INF** – A directory for APK metadata—including signatures.
- **AndroidManifest.xml** – The application manifest in a binary XML formatted file that contains application metadata—for example, its name, version, permissions, etc.
- **classes.dex** – The `classes.dex` file contains the compiled application code in the Dex file format. There can be additional `.dex` files (named `classes2.dex`, etc.) when the application uses multidex.
- **resources.arsc** – This file contains precompiled resources—such as strings, colours, or styles.

Application Information

Both iOS and Android have respective files that contain application configuration information; in iOS, this is the `info.plist` file, and in Android, this is the `AndroidManifest.xml` file.

iOS plist file

Depending on how the application was retrieved from the device/ created, the `plist` file may be in XML or binary (`bplist`) format. If it is in binary format, it can be converted to xml with the following command (on Linux).

```
apt install libplist-utils
plistutil -i Info.plist -o Info_xml.plist
```

As mentioned previously, the plist file contains an assortment of application configuration data, including the following:

- `UsageDescription` – The application permission purpose strings
- `CFBundleURLTypes` – Custom URL schemes
- `NSAppTransportSecurity` – The Application Transport Security (ATS) configuration
- `UTExportedTypeDeclarations` and `UTImportedTypeDeclarations` – Exported and imported custom document types

Android Manifest File

Like iOS, Android APK files also include a file detailing the application configuration. The Android manifest includes information such as:

- Package name and application ID
- Application components
- Intent filters
- Icons and labels information
- Permissions
- Device compatibility information

Retrieving an Application From a Device

In some cases, you may not have access to an application file (i.e., APK or IPS), and you may need to retrieve it from a device. iOS implements a static DRM approach which means the application is encrypted at rest, while Android doesn't have such protection. Nonetheless, it is possible to retrieve both APK and IPA files from running devices.

Android

Retrieving Android applications is a trivial method, as can be seen below:

- Ensure `adb` is enabled on the device by accessing developer settings and configuring adb.
    - Developer settings can be enabled by going to `Settings`, then `About Phone`, `Software Info`, and tapping the device `Build Number` seven times.
- Ensure adb is installed on the host (comes with Android Studio) and is on your path.
- Connect to the devices shell with `adb shell`.
- List all package IDs with `pm list packages | grep <application name>`.
- Retrieve the path to the base APK with `pm path <Package ID>`.
- Exit adb with exit and pull the previously acquired apk file with `adb pull <package base APK path>`.

iOS

As will be mentioned in more detail later in this chapter, iOS applications are encrypted at rest. This means that if an application IPA file was extracted from a device, it would largely not be in a human-readable state. Because of this, techniques such as the below (which require a jailbroken device) can be used to retrieve the application while it is loaded into memory.

- Install Frida locally and on the device.
- Install Frida and `frida-ios-dump` onto your host.
- Identify the process display name with `frida-ps -Uai` and make sure the application is running.
- Run `iproxy 2222 22`.

- Run `python dump.py <Display name>` (mentioned in more detail in a later section).
- Extract the IPA file as if it was a zip file, and inside of the .app folder will be a file named after the application. This is the application MachO binary.

Outside of the above, iOS applications can be retrieved via conventional means (however, they will remain encrypted). In iOS, system applications are stored in the /Applications directory, while user-installed applications are stored in the /private/var/containers directory. Similar to the newer releases of Android, where these paths are appended with random identifiers, this is also the case in iOS, where application paths in these folders receive a random 128-bit UUID as directory names.

iOS applications have two main directories, a bundle directory, and a data directory. These can be identified using the Objection (as described later in this book) env command. The application app folder (which contains the MachO binary) is located in the bundle directory. After this, Objection can be used again to retrieve the app file using the command `file download <remote path> [<local path>]`.

Installing an Application

Sometimes you may be provided an application file(s) to install on a device. This is a trivial process. However, for iOS, one that requires a Jailbroken iOS device.

Android

Below is an example of how to install an application onto an Android device from a machine with adb installed:

- Ensure adb is enabled on the device by accessing developer settings and configuring adb.
  - Developer settings can be enabled by going to `Settings`, then `About Phone`, `Software Info`, and tapping the device `Build Number` seven times.

- Ensure adb is installed on the host (comes with Android Studio) and is on your path.
- `adb install <apk path>`.

iOS

Below is an example of how to install an application onto a jailbroken iOS device from a Linux host PC:

- `sudo apt-get install libimobiledevice`
- `sudo apt-get install ideviceinstaller`
- `ideviceinstaller -i <path to ipa>`

Connecting to the Device CLI

Interacting with a device on the CLI can be critical in understanding its operations and retrieving data and files from a device.

Android

- Ensure adb is enabled on the device by accessing developer settings and configuring adb.
  - Developer settings can be enabled by going to Settings, then About Phone, Software Info, and tapping the device Build Number seven times.
- Ensure adb is installed on the host (comes with Android Studio) and is on your path.
- Connect the device (rooted or standard).
- `adb shell`

iOS

- Connect a jailbroken device.
- Find the device's IP address in network settings.
- `ssh root@<ip>` - password is alpine.

Patching an APK

Sometimes, instead of using dynamic instrumentation, a more permanent change to a target application is required. In this case, the application APK can be patched—this may be done to remove security safeguards, introduce a malicious library, and more. In all cases, it will involve disassembling the application, altering it, and then re-assembling it. Some applications may have safeguards in place to prohibit this, such as checking the certificate the application is signed with, as this process requires that the APK is re-signed.

1. Running the command `apktool d <apk name>` we can disassemble the APK file to SMALI and view the smali file structure in the smali sub-folder.
2. We can then make any changes we need to the Smali. If you are unfamiliar with SMALI, a good method is to write a Java program, compile it, then disassemble it to see what the Smali looks like for that utility.
3. Re-assemble the root folder with `apktool b <folder name> -f`. The repackaged apk is saved in the dist folder.
4. Create certificate: `keytool -genkey -v -keystore custom.keystore -alias mykeyaliasname -keyalg RSA -keysize 2048 -validity 10000`.
5. Sign APK with certificate: `jarsigner -sigalg SHA1withRSA -digestalg SHA1 -keystore custom.keystore -storepass password *.apk mykeyaliasname`. On newer devices, use apksigner. For example, `apksigner sign --ks-key-alias alias_name --ks my.keystore my-app.apk`. When using apksigner, you do not need to use zipalign below.
6. Align APK: `zipalign 4 *.apk repackaged-final.apk`.
7. Install and run the patched application: `adb install repackaged-final.apk`.

Reverse Engineering Applications

Reverse engineering mobile applications follow an almost identical process to reverse engineering any other program or application. However, the acquisition and tooling may be different.

iOS Reverse Engineering

By default, iOS application files (or at least a significant portion) are encrypted and decrypted in memory on an iOS device. While this is the case, it is possible to decrypt these applications. The most common approach for this is retrieving the application while it is in memory. Much tooling exists to this effect, such as the `frida-ios-dump` tooling mentioned in the section FriDump—A Universal Memory Dumping Tool below. While this is the case, this method does require that the device is jailbroken and Frida is present on the device.

Once the iOS IPA, and in turn, MachO file, have been acquired, the MachO file can be loaded into a decompiler/ disassembler of your choosing (i.e., IDA or Ghidra), and you can begin reverse engineering. The MachO file is located inside the extracted IPA file inside the `<application-name>.app` folder. Inside this folder is a file with the naming format of `<application-name>`. This is the MachO file and the file containing the main compiled application codebase.

Android Reverse Engineering

Unlike iOS, Android applications are not encrypted on disk and, in turn, are readily available to be retrieved even if the device isn't rooted. This being the case, adb will need to be enabled on the device so that the device can be communicated with (as discussed earlier in this book).

As with iOS, Android applications are stored in an archive-like format where they can be unzipped, similarly to other archive formats. While this is the case, some information, such as the manifest file, will be incomprehensible unless un-bundled properly. Tooling such as the following exists for the purpose of reverse engineering Android applications:

Option One, via APKTool:

- Run: `apktool d <application name>`
  - Optionally use the -s or --no-src parameters to disassemble the classes.dex file to SMALI. This can then be used for patching the APK, as described earlier in this chapter[2].
- Run `cd <new folder with application name>`
- Run `dex2jar classes.dex`
- Open the new jar file in JDGui

Option Two, via Jadx-GUI:

- Run `jadx-gui <apk name>`
- The below steps are optional:
  - Select `File`, then `save as gradle project`
  - Open the new gradle project in Android Studio

Identifying Security Issues in Mobile Applications

The previous section of this book detailed how to reverse engineer a mobile application and how to begin analysis. As well as this, several sections in the Frida chapter below detail how to perform several attack methods on mobile applications. This section summarises these areas by detailing common vulnerability types present in mobile applications.

iOS common application issues

- **Cookies** – iOS application cookies can be stored in the application's `Library/Cookies/cookies.binarycookies` file or in its keychain. The Objection command ios cookies get can be used to retrieve these.
- **Caches** – `NSURLSession` is a class responsible for providing an API for downloading from and uploading data to endpoints indicated by URLs. It stores data in cache files related to these requests and responses. These

---

2 https://ibotpeaches.github.io/Apktool/documentation/

files can be found in the application's folder under `/Library/Caches/<Bundle Identifier>` or via objection `ios nsurlcredentialstorage dump` or `ios nsuserdefaults get`.

- **Snapshots / Screenshots** – Similar to Android, when the home button is pressed, a screenshot is taken of the current screen, which may contain sensitive information. On non-jailbroken devices, an attacker would need physical access to a device. However, on a jailbroken device, these can be accessed in the application's sandboxed folder at `Library/Caches/Snapshots/` or `Library/SplashBoard/Snapshots`.

- **Keychain** – The iOS keychain was designed to solve the issue of application developers needing to store secret or sensitive data in a secure and encrypted database. The keychain is no longer secure on a jailbroken device and can be dumped with `Objection ios keychain dump`.

- **Broken Cryptography** – Encrypting sensitive data inside an application is a fairly standard approach used in application development. While this is the case, several misconfigurations can lead to broken cryptography and vulnerable data. One of these is where the encryption key is hardcoded or predictable in the codebase and could be retrieved via reverse engineering. The second is when an insecure or deprecated algorithm is in use (such as RC4, MD4, MD5, SHA1, etc.). Cryptography libraries can be automatically monitored using Objection `ios monitor crypt`.

- **Local Authentication** – Local authentication should be performed using the Touch / Face ID framework or via the iOS keychain.

- **Certificate Pinning** – When an application is correctly using certificate pinning, its network connections will only communicate with the receiving server if its certificate is as expected. This can mean that standard man in the middle approaches (such as using Burp Suite to man in the middle traffic) will not be successful. Most SSL pinning can be disabled in a myriad of ways, from using Objection `ios sslpinning disable` or by installing `SSL Kill Switch` or the Burp Mobile Assistant.

- Custom Keyboards – From iOS 8.0, it's possible to install custom keyboards onto iOS devices. This opens up a door for potential information leakage vulnerabilities from typing in sensitive information via a malicious keyboard. Applications can restrict what keyboards can be used on specific aspects of their application.

- **Logs** – As with all programming, many application developers may use logging to debug their applications. When logging is left in a release application, this may lead to sensitive or private information being disclosed.

- **Backups** – iOS performs automatic backups of all data on a device (including application data. This backup can be retrieved using iTunes, Finder, or via the iCloud backup feature. In all cases, it is critical for app developers to ensure that no private or personal data is included in these backups. This can be done by looking for strings in the backup files.

- **Sensitive data in memory** – Similar to the above, it is also important to ensure that the amount of sensitive data in memory is limited. As all sensitive data will be in memory at some stage, it is critical to ensure that this is as brief as possible. A memory dump of an application can be achieved via Objection or FriDump.

Android common application issues

- **Exploiting exported activities** – When an activity is exported, it can be invoked from external applications or via adb. This means that if there is an authentication mechanism before a user would normally be able to reach an activity, but it is exported, then a malicious actor would be able to call the activity directly. This can be done using Drozer, or an activity can also be called from adb `adb shell am start -n com.example.demo/com.example.test.MainActivity`. This is also the case for services and broadcast receivers, but as services often receive data, the decompiled code will need to be reviewed for an understanding of how it can be exploited.

- **Insecure data storage** – Sensitive data should not be stored in the external storage, and when stored in the internal storage, the `MODE_WORLD_READBALE` and `MODE_WORLD_WRITABLE` modes should be limited as much as possible.

- **Broken cryptography** – Encrypting sensitive data inside of an application is a standard approach used in application development. While this is the case, there are several misconfigurations that can lead to broken cryptography and vulnerable data. One of these is where the encryption key is hardcoded or predictable in the codebase and could be retrieved via reverse engineering. The second of these is when an insecure or deprecated algorithm is in use (such as RC4, MD4, MD5, SHA1, etc.).

- **Sensitive data in memory** – Similar to iOS, it is also important to ensure that the amount of sensitive data in memory is limited. As all sensitive data will be in memory at some stage, it is critical to ensure that this is as brief as possible. A memory dump of an application can be achieved via `objection` or `fridump`.

- **Tapjacking** – Tapjacking is an attack where a malicious application overlays a target application and modifies its UI to make the user believe they are interacting with the normal application. For a malicious application to achieve this, the target application will need to have an exported activity. If it has any permissions, the malicious application will need to share them. Touch filtering can be disabled to limit touch events when a view is covered by the `setFilterTouchesWhenObscured(boolean)` method. Quark can be used with the `-exploit-apk` flag to check if an application may be vulnerable to this attack.

- **Task hijacking** – Is the process of having a specially crafted malicious application that has its `android:taskAffinity` set to the same affinity as the vulnerable app. In the scenario where the malicious application is already on the task stack and has been opened, and the vulnerable activity is attempted to be opened, the malicious application is switched to instead.

Application Integrity for iOS and Android

- Applications should be obfuscated to increase the labour required in reverse engineering by a malicious actor
- Sensitive applications should perform their own root[3], emulation, and jailbreak detection checks

---

[3] https://developer.android.com/training/safetynet/attestation

CHAPTER FOUR

DYNAMIC INSTRUMENTATION OF MOBILE APPLICATIONS WITH FRIDA

Dynamic instrumentation is the process of modifying a program's flow during execution; this is commonly performed by modifying a program's instruction set in memory. This chapter focuses on the Frida dynamic instrumentation toolset and how it can be used to hook Android and iOS applications.

What This Section Is

- An introduction to the concepts behind dynamic and static instrumentation.
- An introduction to dynamic instrumentation with Frida on Android and iOS.
- A guide on how to install, hook with, and perform other actions on mobile devices using Frida and related tooling.

What This Section Is Not

- A detailed look at the lower-level workings of Frida.

Tools Used Throughout This Section

- Frida – https://frida.re/
- Frida iOS Dump – https://github.com/AloneMonkey/frida-ios-dump
- FriDump – https://github.com/Nightbringer21/fridump
- Objection – https://github.com/sensepost/objection
- Magisk Manager – https://github.com/topjohnwu/Magisk/releases

What Is Instrumentation

Dynamic instrumentation is the process of modifying the instructions of a binary program while it executes. There are two types of instrumentation, dynamic and static. Where static instrumentation is performed by patching or modifying an application before execution, and dynamic involves the modification of the application at runtime and in memory. A visual example of dynamic instrumentation can be seen in Figure 6 - Dynamic Instrumentation Explained.

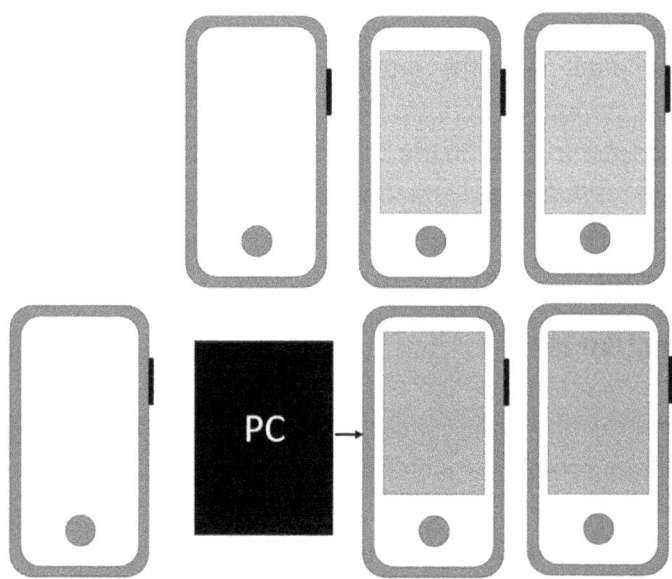

Figure 6 - Dynamic Instrumentation Explained

Normal Program Execution

In this example, the expected normal execution of the target application displays a grey rectangle to the screen after launch.

Dynamically Instrumented Application

In this example, our application is hooked with a dynamic instrumentation toolkit (from our PC) where it is able to modify program flow and memory of the application to make it display a blue rectangle to the screen instead.

Frida Architecture

Frida is an example of a dynamic instrumentation toolkit that is comprised of two components (a server and a client) and can be used to dynamically instrument and hook processes running on Windows, MacOS, Linux, iOS, and more.

Frida on the client can be controlled using either Python or C APIs. This functionality solely controls what happens on the client and how the agent (also known as the server) will be communicated with. Frida core on the agent then injects QuickJS into the target process, executing the written JavaScript. This JavaScript is then run on the device in the target process. Frida supports a bi-directional communication channel for getting information to and from the client and agent. A visual representation of this can be seen in Figure 7 - Frida bi-directional communication.

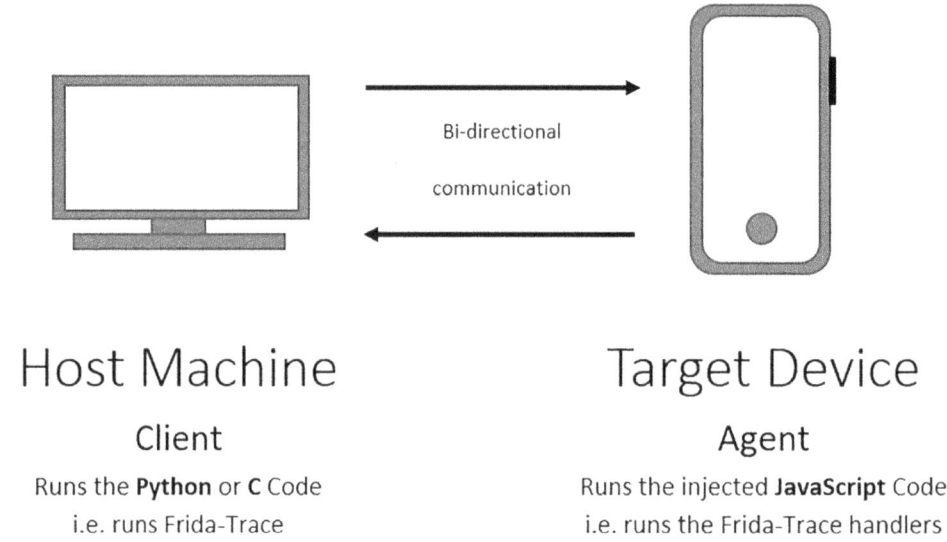

Host Machine

Client

Runs the **Python** or **C** Code
i.e. runs Frida-Trace

Target Device

Agent

Runs the injected **JavaScript** Code
i.e. runs the Frida-Trace handlers

Figure 7 - Frida bi-directional communication

Installation

As previously discussed, Frida has two elements a server and a client. The client should be installed locally on a PC, and the server will need to be installed on the target device (or patched into the desired application).

Android

- Download the Frida client for your OS version onto your PC
- Download the Frida server for your specific rooted device and install it (this can be done by pushing the binary onto the device, setting the appropriate permissions with `chmod`, and running the binary). An application can also be patched with the Frida server to achieve a similar effect on non-rooted devices—this can be done manually or by using Objection, with `objection patchapk -s <application name>.apk --enable-debug`.
- Retrieve a list of processes/ gadgets running on the device with `frida-ps -Uai`

- Develop a script (or use Frida-trace, etc.) to interact with the running processes/ gadgets. See page 45 for examples

iOS

- Download the Frida client for your OS version onto your PC
- Ensure you have Cydia installed on your jailbroken iOS device. Add Frida to your Cydia repositories via: `Manage -> Sources -> Edit -> Add` and enter `https://build.frida.re`. Frida is also able to instrument debuggable apps automatically as of Frida 12.7.12
- Retrieve a list of processes/ gadgets running on the device with `frida-ps -Uai`
- Develop a script (or use Frida-trace, etc.) to interact with the running processes/ gadgets. See page 45 for examples

Frida Trace

Frida-Trace is a Frida utility that is commonly the first port-of-call for people using Frida. It allows for the tracing of function calls, modification of their parameters and return values, and much more powerful operations. As can be seen below, Frida-trace takes a filter for the function name you want to trace and has handlers for modifying these values. These handlers can be seen when it first runs and are modifiable JavaScript files. In addition to this, it also allows for tracing objective-c functions for iOS and Android native functions.

Android

The below example traces all SQLite calls and aggregates where the databases being traced is.

- `frida-trace -U -i "open*" -I "*sqlite*" -f "com.android.chrome"`
- `cd __handlers__/libsqlite.so/ ; ls`
- To modify the handler: `nano sqlite3_open_v2.js`

Example output:

```
open(pathname="/data/user/0/com.android.chrome/app_chrome/
Default/Offline Pages/metadata/OfflinePages.db", flags=0xa8042)
```

iOS

The below example traces network traffic requests.

- `frida-trace -m "-[NSURLRequest initWithURL:]" -U -f "com.ios.demo"`
- `cd __handlers__/libsqlite.so/ ; ls`
- To modify the handler: `nano __NSURLRequest_initWithURL_cache_1902507d.js`

Frida-Trace Reference

- **-f** Launches the application when run, rather than the default behavior that attaches to the application
- **-U** Connects Frida with the connected USB device
- **-I** MODULE, --include-module=MODULE | include MODULE
- **-X** MODULE, --exclude-module=MODULE | exclude MODULE
- **-i** FUNCTION, --include=FUNCTION | include [MODULE]![FUNCTION]
- **-x** FUNCTION, --exclude=FUNCTION | exclude [MODULE]![FUNCTION]
- **-a** MODULE!OFFSET, --add=MODULE!OFFSET | add MODULE!OFFSET
- **-T**, --include-imports | include program's imports
- **-t** MODULE, --include-module-imports=MODULE | include MODULE imports
- **-m** OBJC_METHOD, --include-objc-method=OBJC_METHOD | include OBJC_METHOD
- **-M** OBJC_METHOD, --exclude-objc-method=OBJC_METHOD | exclude OBJC_METHOD
- **-j** JAVA_METHOD, --include-java-method=JAVA_METHOD | include JAVA_METHOD
- **-J** JAVA_METHOD, --exclude-java-method=JAVA_METHOD | exclude JAVA_METHOD

- **-s** DEBUG_SYMBOL, --include-debug-symbol=DEBUG_SYMBOL | include DEBUG_SYMBOL

Running Frida Scripts

There are two main components of Frida scripts, the Python, which is used to communicate with your local system (and initiate communication with a device), and the JavaScript, which runs on the device in the target process. Several bridges and APIs exist for communication between the two languages.

Python Component Example

Here package_name defines the name of the target application and java_script_code_ path defines the name of the JavaScript file being run.

```python
import frida
package_name = "application_reverse_domain_notation"
java_script_code_path = "javascript-Frida-code.js"
def my_message_handler(message, payload):
    print (message)
    print (payload)


# Opens a session with the device/ process/ gaget
session = frida.get_usb_device().attach(package_name)


# Reads and executes the javascript code
with open(java_script_code_path) as f:
    script = session.create_script(f.read())
script.on("message", my_message_handler)
script.load()


# prevent the python script from terminating
input()
```

JavaScript Component Example

Ensure to replace com.example.app.MainActivity and function_name with the class and function path names you're looking to hook.

```
Java.perform(function () {
    var ClassName = Java.use('com.example.app.MainActivity');
    console.log("Fond ClassName Successfully!");
    // Replace function_name with target function name
    ClassName.function_name.implementation=function(){
        console.log("Entered Function")
});
```

Frida Script Examples

The below examples show several use cases for using Frida scripts—from hooking and accessing the variables in use in a class's constructor and functions to calling a function with custom parameters.

Hook Constructor

Ensure to replace com.example.application.main with the class path and name of the constructor you're looking to hook. Ensure to replace android.content.Context with the path to the variable types the constructor takes (a tip here is that Frida will return an error with the correct paths if they are incorrect).

```
Java.perform(function () {
    var ClassName = Java.use('com.example.application.main');
    console.log("Found ClassName Successfully!");
    ClassName.$init.overload('android.content.Context').
    implementation=function(context){
    console.log("In Constructor")
    }
});
```

Hook Function

Ensure to replace `function_name` and `com.example.application.main` with the name of the function and classes you're looking to hook. Ensure to replace x,y with the appropriate number of values for the parameters the function takes.

```
console.log("Script loaded successfully ");
Java.perform(function function_name(){
console.log("Inside java perform function");
var my_class = Java.use("com.example.application.main");
my_class.function_name.implementation = function(x,y){
      console.log( "inside function");
   }});
```

Initialize a Call

Ensure to replace `com.example.application.main` with the name of the class you're looking to initialise and to replace ("param1","param2") with the correct number of and values you wish to initialise the class with.

```
Java.perform(function () {
    var className = Java.use("com.example.application.main");
    var uploadREquestIstance = className.$new("param1","param2");
    console.log("Finished Initialisation")
});
```

Example initialize and calling a function

Ensure to replace `com.example.application.main` and `function_name` with the name and path for the class and function being called. Secondly ensure to replace ("param1","param2") with the correct number of and values you wish to initialise the class with.

```
Java.perform(function () {
    var className = Java.use("com.example.application.main");
    console.log("Finished Initialisation")
});

//Find an instance of the class and call function.
Java.choose("com.example.application.main", {
    onMatch: function (instance) {
        console.log("found class instance");
        instance.function_name("param1", " param2");
    },
});
```

FriDump – A Universal Memory Dumping Tool

Identifying plain text strings in memory may not form a part of standard day-to-day testing of mobile applications. That being the case, it is an ideal way to identify aspects of a running application that may have been overlooked. FriDump utilizes Frida and so requires either a rooted Android device or a patched application and, for iOS, a Jailbroken device.

Android

- Download the Frida client for your OS version onto your PC.
- Ensure the Frida server is successfully installed and running on your device (as described previously)
- Download and install FriDump from their GitHub page listed at the start of this chapter.
- Ensure the application is running and identify the process name you wish to dump the memory of with `frida-ps -Uai`.
- Run `python3 fridump.py -U <process name/ reverse domain notation> -s`

iOS

- Download the Frida client for your OS version onto your PC.
- Ensure the Frida server is successfully installed and running on your device (as described previously).
- Download and install FriDump from their GitHub page listed at the start of this chapter.
- Ensure the application is running and identify the process name you wish to dump the memory of with `frida-ps -Uai`.
- Run `python3 fridump.py -U <process name/ reverse domain notation> -s`.

When the `-s` parameter is used a single file containing all the identified strings in memory will be created. This can be used for identifiying if sensative information is being leaked in memory.

Objection

Objection is a dynamic instrumentation toolkit that wraps around Frida and supports Android and iOS. It allows for a collection of pre-configured testing methods such as subverting SSL pinning, subverting root or jailbreak detection, and dumping sensitive data.

Installing Objection on iOS

- Download the Frida client for your OS version onto your PC.
- Ensure the Frida server is successfully installed and running on your device (as described previously).
- Download and install Objection (this can be downloaded from the website listed at the start of this chapter).
- Identify the application reverse domain notation name (next to the application/ process name) with `frida-ps -Uai`.
- Connect objection to the application with `objection -g <reverse domain notation name> explore`.

Objection iOS Command Examples

Disable Certificate Pinning	`ios sslpinning disable --quiet`
Dump The Application Keychain	`ios keychain dump`
Check Cookies Datastore	`ios cookies get`
NSUserDefaulrs Datastore	`ios nsuserdefaults get`
NSURL Credential Storage Datastore	`ios nsurlcredentialstorage dump`
Circumvent Jailbreak	`ios jailbreak disable`
Memory Dump	`memory dump all`
Monitor Crypto Libraries	`ios monitor crypt`

Table 5 - Objection iOS Examples

Installing Objection on Android

- Download the Frida client for your OS version onto your PC.
- Ensure the Frida server is successfully installed and running on your device (as described previously).
- Download and install Objection (this can be downloaded from the website listed at the start of this chapter).
- Identify the application reverse domain notation name (next to the application/ process name) with frida-ps –Uai.
- Connect objection to the application with objection -g <reverse domain notation name> explore.

Objection Android Command Examples

Disable Certificate Pinning	`android sslpinning disable`
Disable Root Detection	`android root disable`
Simulate Root On The Device	`android root simulate`
Enable screenshot	`android ui FLAG_SECURE false`
Take screenshot	`android ui screenshot /tmp/screenshot`
Keystore	`android keystore list`
Memory Dump	`memory dump all`

Table 6 - Objection Android Example

CHAPTER FIVE

OPERATING SYSTEM INTERNALS

Understanding the internals of modern mobile devices can provide insight into their workings and how to successfully reverse engineer and exploit their systems or applications. Operating system internals can be defined as the following:

> *An understanding of the low-level inner workings of an operating system. Commonly involving understanding the Kernel, Hardware abstraction layer, and the platform.*

What This Section Is

- A review of key components seen across all computing architectures.
- A review of the iOS and Android architectures and their key components.

What This Section Is Not

- A detailed look at every component that makes up the Android and iOS systems.

Tools Used Throughout This Section

- No specific tools are mentioned in this chapter.

FUNDAMENTAL CONCEPTS

Applications / Programs

Developed by third parties, designed to run on the target OS to extend functionality.

Inter Process Communication (IPC)

IPC relates to how a process communicates/ shares data with other processes on the device. This is typically done in a client/ server model where a server is initialized, and client processes connects to the server to begin communication.

Kernel

The kernel is responsible for low-level tasks such as disk, memory, and task management and will generally have complete control over the system. Programs and other services can utilize the Kernel by making a request commonly called a System Call.

Hardware Abstraction Layer (HAL)

The HAL allows for abstract differences in hardware implementations (e.g., two devices having separate camera hardware) and allows for a standard API for accessing hardware of the same type.

User Mode

A processor switches between two modes depending on what code it's running. In User mode, the executing code has no ability to directly access hardware or reference memory. Code running in user mode must delegate to system APIs to access hardware or memory.

Kernel Mode

A processor switches between two modes depending on what code it's running. In Kernel mode, the executing code has complete and unrestricted access to the underlying hardware. It can execute any CPU instruction and reference any memory address. Kernel mode is generally reserved for the operating system's lowest-level, most trusted functions.

Sandboxing

Some operating systems implement sandboxing at varying levels of the OS. For example, in Android, each application runs under a different Linux user, prohibiting cross interaction between applications.

ANDROID ARCHITECTURE

A form of embedded Linux. Android incorporates an entire software stack for mobile devices, including: The Android Open-Source Project (AOSP - the Open-Source component), Linux Kernel, Platform, Vendor, Carrier components, and third-party applications. A visual representation of the architecture can be seen in Figure 8 - Android Architecture.

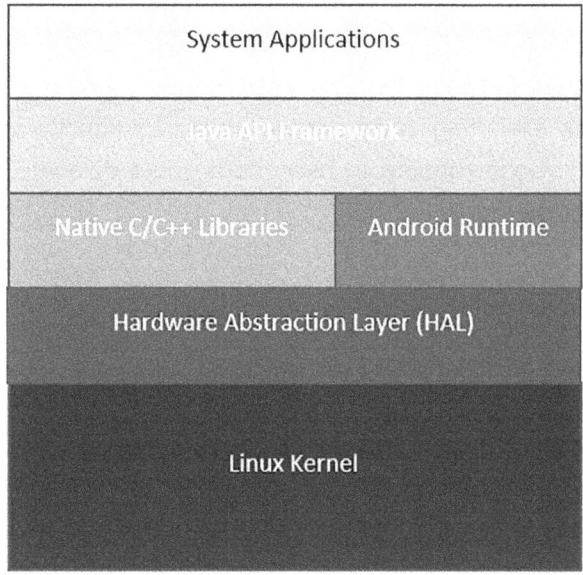

Figure 8 - Android Architecture

Dalvik Virtual Machine

When an Android application has compiled an aspect of the created file (APK) contains a .dex file (Dalvik Bytecode). This bytecode is run inside a Dalvik Virtual Machine (on newer versions of Android, there are additional layers of optimization involved). Unlike a Java VM, the DVM is register-based.

Some Android Applications may need to escape the VM—usually to access hardware. Dalvik, therefore, allows the inclusion of native libraries (ELF shared objects) in application code through the Java Native Interface (JNI).

Sandboxing

Android runs under a multi-user Linux system which means that each application and its storage runs under a separate user. This means that under normal circumstances, applications cannot read another application's data or internal storage.

Bionic

Unlike other Linux distributions, which use GLibC (`libc.so`) as their core runtime, Android uses a proprietary C-runtime library called Bionic. The choice of this comes down to both legal issues (GLibC comes with specific restrictions) as well as having a more lightweight option. Additional considerations include:

- Streamlined system call support
- No support for System V IPC
- Limited C++ support
- No support for Locales and/or wide characters

Hardware Abstraction Layer (HAL)

Due to Android needing to run on a myriad of different devices (all with varying hardware), a HAL is required. In turn, The Hardware Abstraction Layer defines what an abstract camera, GPS, sensor, etc., looks like and can do in Android. HAL binaries can be found in `/vendor/lib/hw or /system/lib/hw`.

Daemons

Android uses multiple daemons in the background for performing varying levels of functionality, including:

- **adbd** – providing the server functionality for the Android Debug Bridge (ADB).

- **healthd** – Periodically services device health, including battery properties.
- **lmkd** – Low Memory Killer, which builds off OOM (Out of Memory Killer) and automatically kills tasks during memory pressure.

Binder

Binder is one of Android's main IPC mechanisms, which all applications can open. Android services register with Binder, and clients can connect to them with the help of *servcemanager*.

Zygote

Dalvik VMs are created by Zygote (zai·gowt). Zygote is launched by the Android runtime at startup with the first virtual machine, and all shared java classes and resources. When a new application wants to launch, a new Zygote process is forked, and the application is bound to the thread of the new process.

IOS ARCHITECTURE

IOS is the mobile operating system developed by Apple. Primarily used for iPhones, iPads, and the iPod touch. Second to Android, it is one of the most globally popular mobile operating systems.

Like Android and other operating systems, iOS' architecture is layer[4] based. A visual representation of the architecture can be seen in Figure 9 - iOS Architecture[5] below.

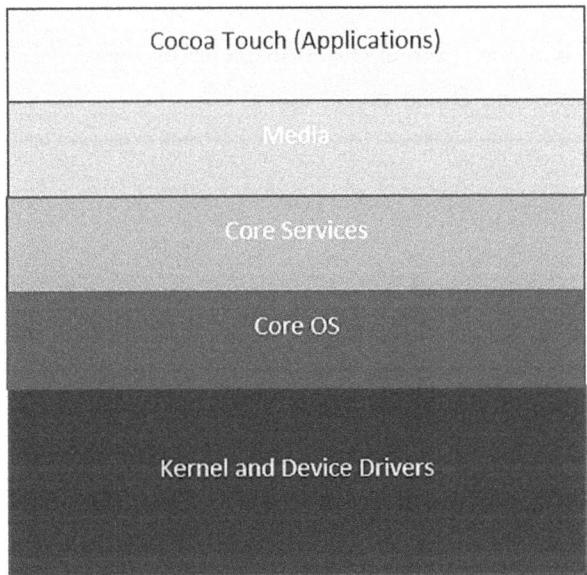

Figure 9 - iOS Architecture

Cocoa Touch

Cocoa Touch functions as an abstraction layer that provides various libraries for iOS developers. Cocoa Touch is the top layer of the iOS architecture and provides intrinsic functionality such as touch-based controls and multitasking[6].

---

4   https://intellipaat.com/blog/tutorial/ios-tutorial/ios-architecture/

5   https://intellipaat.com/blog/tutori

6   al/ios-tutorial/ios-architecture/spoint.com/apple-ios-architecture" https://www.tutorialspoint.com/apple-ios-architecture

Media

This provides iOS and, in turn, iOS applications with all of the functionality required to perform multimedia operations—such as video, animation, graphic, and audio functions. Containing frameworks such as: the Core Audio Framework, Core Text framework, and the Core Image framework.

Core Services

This layer functions as another abstraction layer, however, this time between the above layers and the Core OS Layer.

Core OS

The bottom-most layer sits above the Kernel and Device drivers. This layer is responsible for managing memory, the file system, network communications, and other operating system-related tasks.

CHAPTER SIX

BASEBAND

Over the years, there has been a steady rise in mobile devices operating worldwide. In 2021 this number stood at almost 15 million. While the architecture of modern mobile devices varies from manufacturer to manufacturer, almost all of these 15 million devices will use a baseband implementation in one form or another—as it is this technology that allows for radio communication via cell networks and base stations.

As this technology underpins so many devices, is used by millions, and is quite complex, it is pertinent for security researchers to understand the technology so that vulnerabilities can be identified and defence mitigations can be put in place.

What This Section Is

- An introduction to the background and fundamental principles of baseband reverse engineering and vulnerability research.

- A method for starting reverse engineering on modern baseband implementations.

What This Section Is Not

- A list of zero-days or exploits for modern baseband implementations
- A detailed guide on specific baseband implementations.

Tools Used Throughout This Section

- A disassembler (i.e., Ghidra or IDA) – https://ghidra-sre.org/ or https://hex-rays.com/ida-pro/
- AFL++ – https://github.com/AFLplusplus/AFLplusplus

Baseband Implementations and Devices

There are many different baseband chip manufacturers. This section details a selection of these, detailing their practicality and supporting information.

To better understand the distribution of baseband chips, Figure 10 - Baseband revenue share details the market share of the main chipset manufacturers in 2020[7].

---

[7] https://www.statista.com/statistics/427073/cellular-baseband-processor-supplier-share/

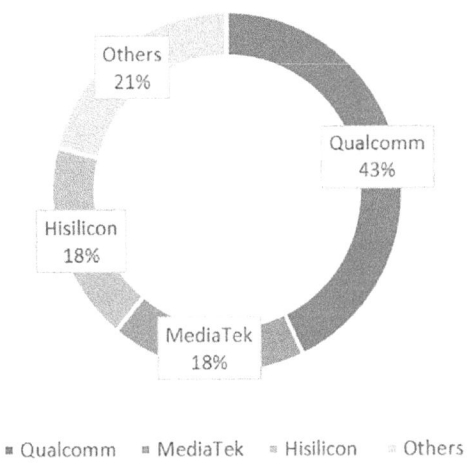

Figure 10 - Baseband revenue share

Shannon

NAME	CATEGORY
SHANNON	Samsung devices not located in the US.

Table 7 - Shannon Baseband

Shannon is Samsung's baseband implementation and is present in Samsung devices outside of the US. Inside the US, Samsung uses the Qualcomm baseband implementation. The reason why Shannon uses Qualcomm in the US is fairly complex. However, it comes down to a business agreement between Samsung and Qualcomm, where in turn, for shipping phones with Qualcomm processors into the US, Samsung would fabricate Snapdragon processors. In addition to this, as CDMA is used heavily in the US and Qualcomm holds critical CDMA patents, Samsung would have to pay additional royalties to ship devices into the US.

Balong

NAME	CATEGORY
BALONG	Modern HiSilicon (Huawei) devices

Table 8 - Balong Baseband

In 2007 Huawei began the development of their first proprietary baseband chips, taking over from their dependence on Qualcomm chips. In 2010 Huawei launched its first TD-LTE baseband chip, the Balong 700. The chips are fabricated by HiSilicon, an organization wholly owned by Huawei.

Qualcomm

Name	Category
QUALCOMM	A range of devices

Table 9 - Qualcomm Baseband

Qualcomm is a large chip manufacturer providing licenses to use their chips to a wide range of device manufacturers. This list of devices includes: US-base Samsung devices, older Huawei devices, OnePlus, Google Pixels, some iPhones, and more.

MediaTek

NAME	CATEGORY
MEDIATEK	A range of devices

Table 10 - MediaTek Baseband

Covering a large portion of devices from other regions, including lower grade entry models of smartphones. MediaTek baseband chips are included in device models such as Alcatel, Oppo, Tecno, and iTel.

CELL TOWERS, BASE STATIONS, AND RADIO NETWORKS

Cell Towers

Land areas supplied with radio services are broken down into hexagonal cells (or other regular shapes) to provide radio connectivity to mobile devices. Within these land areas, users of mobile devices can seamlessly switch between cells. Each of these cells is assigned with multiple frequencies (f1 – f6), which have corresponding radio base stations (The same frequencies can be used in non-adjacent cells). Cell towers can also use a directional signal to improve reception in higher-traffic areas.

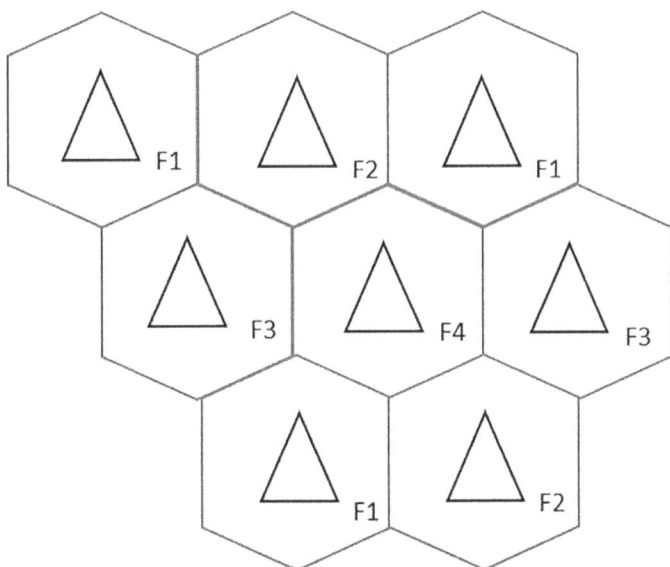

Figure 11 - Simplified Cell Tower View

Figure 11 - Simplified Cell Tower View shows a simplified view of cells, each with its own assigned frequency.

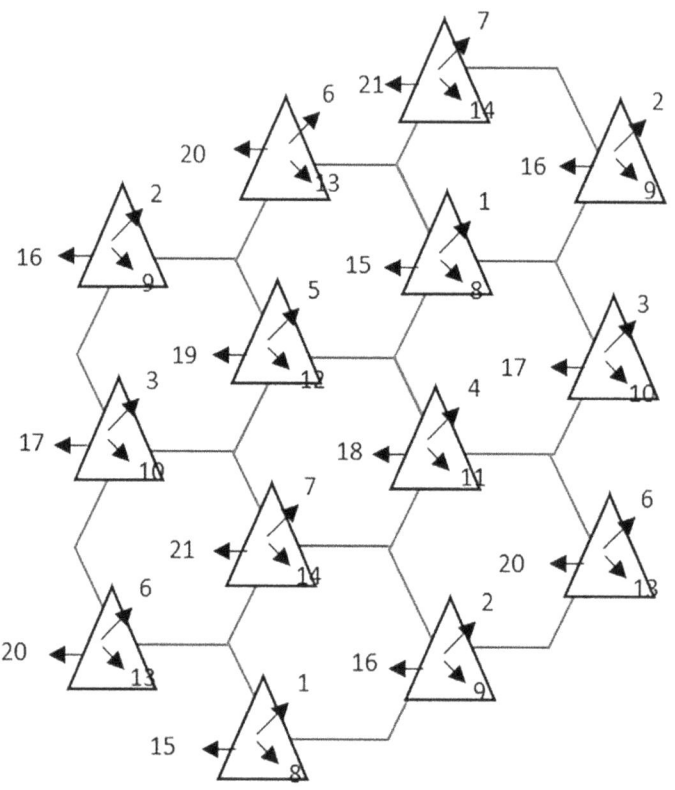

Figure 12 - Directional frequencies

Figure 12 - Directional frequencies show another view of a cell network. In this example, directional frequencies are being used.

Base Stations

In contrast, a base station provides the connection between mobile phones and the wider telephone network. These base stations are commonly located inside of a cell. In Global System for Mobile Communications (GSM) networks, the correct term is Base Transceiver Station (BTS). However, they are colloquially referred to as "mobile phone masts" or "base stations".

User Equipment

User Equipment (UE) is the term used to refer to a mobile handset that connects to a radio network. Depending on the radio network being used, this terminology may differ and is sometimes referred to as the Mobile Station (MS). This device does not necessarily have to be a mobile phone and instead can be any device connected to the radio network.

Radio Networks: GSM and CDMA

To communicate with cell towers and the wider network, a mobile device needs to support the technology behind a radio network. The two most popular radio networks are Global System for Mobile Communication (GSM) and Code Division Multiple Access (CDMA). Table 11 - GSM and CDMA summary details a comparison between these two technologies.

GSM has become the global standard for mobile communications worldwide, having a market share of over 90% and operating in over 193 countries. In contrast, CDMA holds a significantly lower market share and is only used in a small subset of countries. Figure 13 - GSM and CDMA prevalence details a high-level view of countries where GSM and CDMA are used—this is an approximation.

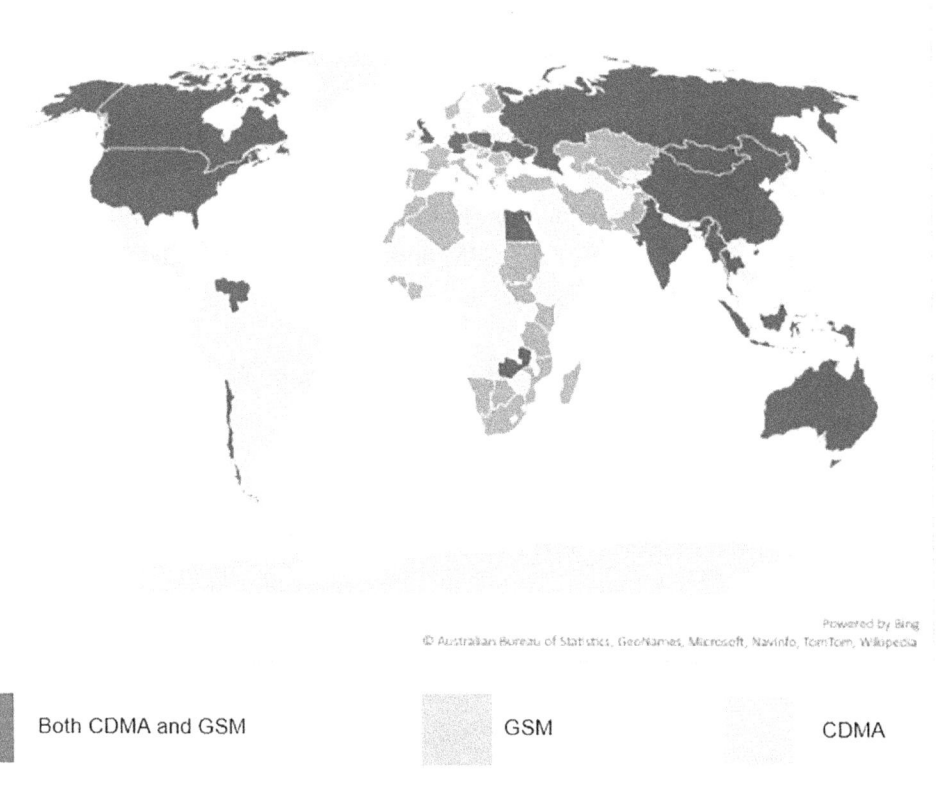

Both CDMA and GSM   GSM   CDMA

Figure 13 - GSM and CDMA prevalence

	GSM	CDMA
Full form	Global System for Mobile communication.	Code Division Multiple Access.
Technology used	FDMA(Frequency division multiple access) and TDMA (Time division multiple access).	CDMA(Code division multiple access).
Availability	GSM is widely used globally	CDMA is available in a smaller subset of countries
Data speed rate	42Mbps in HSPA (3G).	3.6Mbps in CDMA.
Data and voice	GSM supports transmitting data and voice simultaneously	This is not supported by CDMA
Customer Information	Stored in a SIM card.	Stored on device

Table 11 - GSM and CDMA summary

Generations of Mobile Technology

Mobile technology has come along heaps and bounds since its inception. This section breaks down some of the key milestones during that journey, from the early days of mobile phone technology to modern 5G implementations.

First Generation | 1G

Being reliant on analogue radio systems meant that 1G devices could only communicate via conventional phone calling. 1G brought the first cell towers with it, being introduced in Japan in 1979 and the USA in 1980. At this time, encryption had not been introduced, so network traffic could be intercepted with ease.

Second Generation | 2G

Introduced in 1991, 2G utilized a digital signal which improved security and also allowed for SMS and MMS messages. Later in 1997, when GPRS was introduced, email could also be sent.

Third Generation | 3G

With 3G came greater support for faster speeds. This increase in speed allowed for video calling, file sharing, and accessing the wider internet. 3G networks are still used in 2022, commonly when 4G+ networks are not available.

Fourth Generation | 4G

Five times faster than 3G, 4G came with general quality of life improvements related to its speed. Primarily allowing for higher quality calls, faster internet access, high-speed gaming, and more.

Fifth Generation | 5G

Similar to the advancement to 4G from 3G, 5G comes with greatly improved speeds. As well as being used in mobile devices, 5G is also common place and anticipated to be used in internet of things (IoT), smart city, and smart vehicle systems.

Devices leveraging a 5G radio have two main deployment types: Non standalone mode (NSA) and Standalone Mode (SA). NSA mode utilizes the new 5G radio. However, uses the old 4G network and network components. SA mode fully implements the 5G radio and 5G network specifications.

Table 12 - Mobile technology summary explains the development of these technologies further.

Mobile Technology Summary and Future

Features	1G	2G	3G	4G	5G
Release (approximate)	1979	1991	2002	2010	2015
Technology	AMPS, NMT, TACS	GSM	WCDMA	LTE, WiMax	MIMO, mm Waves
Frequency	30 KHz	1.8 GHz	1.6 – 2 GHz	2 – 8 GHz	3 – 30 GHz
Bandwidth	2 kbps	14.4 – 64kbps	2 Mbps	2000 Mbps to 1 Gbps	1 Gbps and higher

Table 12 - Mobile technology summary

Figure 14 - 5G forecast adoption details a chart from Statista referencing the Ericsson Mobility Report as forecast in June 2021, defining that global 5G adoption is to hit over two billion in 2024.

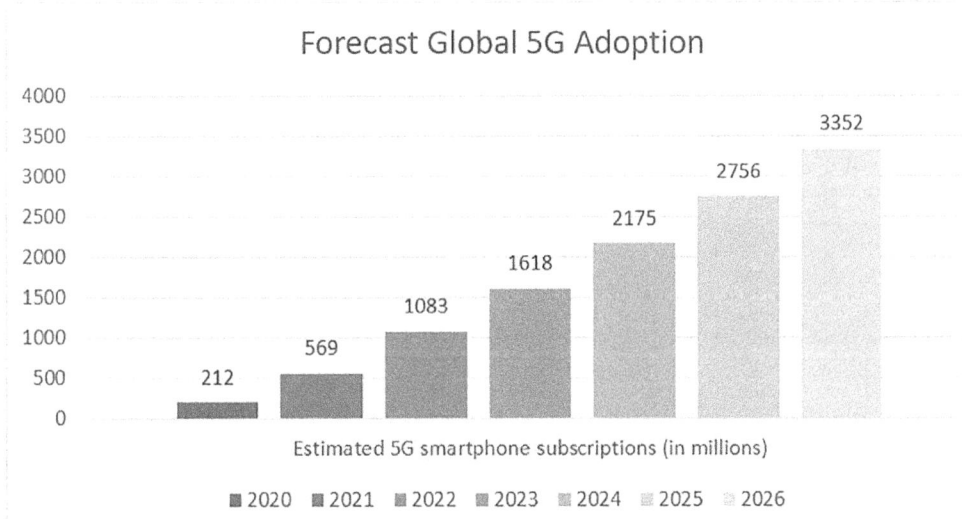

Figure 14 - 5G forecast adoption

Baseband Processor

A baseband processor manages all the radio functions as part of GSM or CDMA (or both) communications, converting digital data into radio frequency signals and vice versa. On modern mobile devices, the baseband processor is commonly segregated from the application processor (AP) that manages the UI (i.e., runs Android or iOS) and other components. The baseband processor will commonly run a Real Time Operating System (RTOS), function independently of the AP, and communicate via a Radio Interface Layer.

Figure 15 - Baseband architecture details this further. This segregation between the AP and BP is commonly done for:

- **Radio Performance and Reliability**.
- **Code execution separation** – stopping trivial attacks and vulnerabilities making their way from the baseband stack to the application stack.
- **Legal Issues** – where some jurisdictions require communication software stacks to be certified.

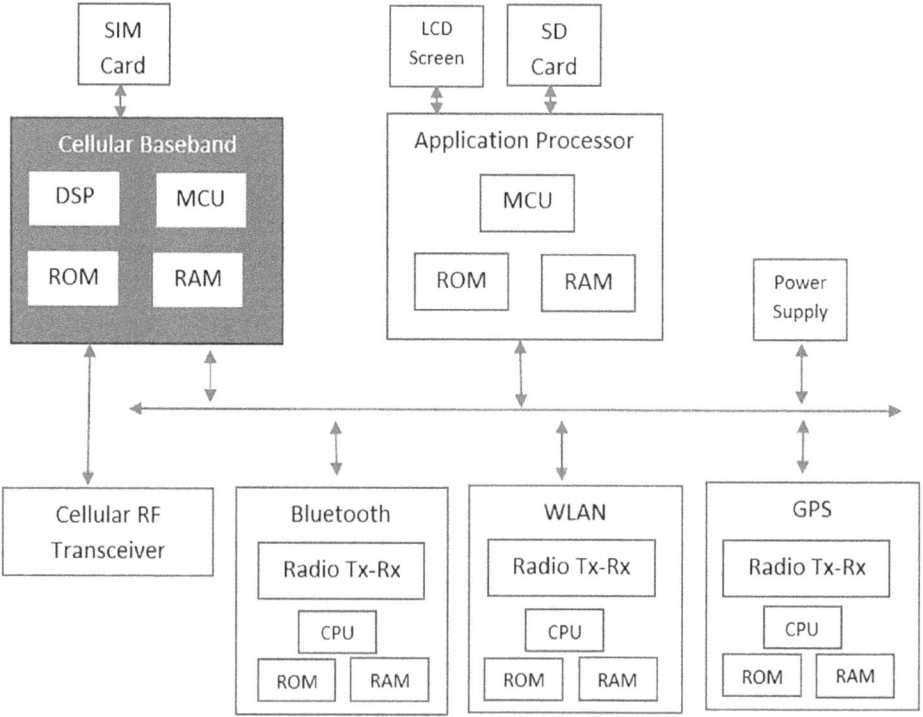

Figure 15 - Baseband architecture

RTOS Tasks

All modern baseband implementations operate a Real Time Operating System (RTOS) as their OS. An RTOS is intended to serve real-time applications that process data as it comes in, typically without buffer delays.

The main unit of execution in an RTOS is a task. Tasks can be created, deleted, resumed, suspended, interrupted by other tasks, and delayed by the task itself. This can be seen in Figure 16 - RTOS task lifecycle.

Each task has its own set of context registers, including a stack. Tasks are also assigned a priority, ranging from 0 (the highest priority) to 255 (the lowest priority). This is visually represented in Figure 17 - RTOS task lifecycle.

Task Lifecycle

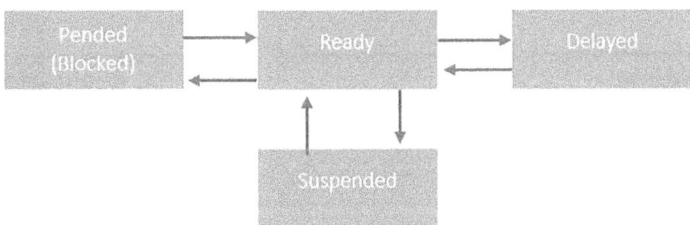

Figure 16 - RTOS task lifecycle

In Figure 17 - RTOS task lifecycle, it can be seen how Task A is executing. Then to move to a higher priority task (Task B), the Interrupt Service Routine (ISR) is used to signal the new task.

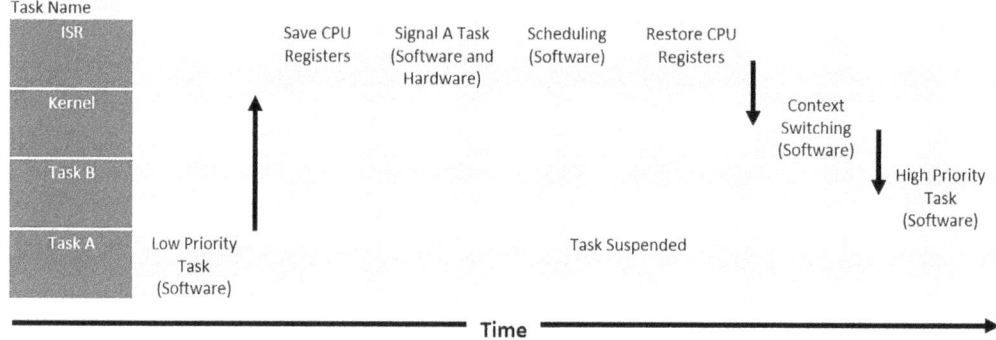

Figure 17 - RTOS task lifecycle

Baseband Protocol Stack

As with any other network implementation, the baseband network stack is layered and distantly aligned with the OSI-Model. This similarity can be seen in the following table, where the OSI model is compared with the baseband GSM implementation. This can be seen in Table 13 - GSM compared to the OSI model.

OSI Model		Realisation In GSM
Application Layer	*Tasks of the user*	
Presentation Layer		
Session Layer	*Tasks of the fixed network*	
Transport Layer		
Network Layer	*Tasks of the GSM network*	Call Control
		Mobility Management
		Radio Resource Manager
Data Link Layer		Segmentation / Concatenation
		Acknowledgement
Physical Layer		Forward Error Correction
		Channel Coding
		Modulation

Table 13 - GSM compared to the OSI model

In addition to this similarity with other layer-based network models, there are several unique protocols to the GSM baseband implementation. A subset of these can be seen in Figure 18 - GSM network layers.

- **Connection Management (CM)** – This functionality is key in establishing, controlling, and processing calls.
- **Mobility Management (MM)** – A core GSM component, allowing a UE to connect to a BTS. In turn, the MM is used to report the location of the device to the cell network so that the most applicable cell and BTS are used for communication.
- **Radio Resource Management (RRM)** – Managing radio resources, transmission, and co-channel interference, this utility is also instrumental in efficiently optimising the use of the radio infrastructure.
- **LAPDm** – The layer 2 component utilised between the UE and BTS.
- **Session Management (SM)** – Responsible for forwarding data between GPRS subscribers and the internet.
- **Subnetwork Dependent Convergence Protocol (SNDCP)** – Providing compression and segmentation services to IPv4 and IPv6 services.
- **Radio/ Logical Link Control (RLC/ LLC)** – Providing the synchronization, flow control, and error checking functions for the data link layer.
- **Non-Access Stratum (NAS)** – This element establishes and maintains communication sessions while a UE moves location.
- **Radio Resource Control (RRC)** – Controlling and configuring the user planes based on network status and facilitating radio resource strategies to be implemented.
- **Packet Data Convergence Protocol (PDCP)** – Incorporates transfer of both user and control plane data as well as ciphering and integrity protection functions.

Figure 18 - GSM network layers shows how these protocols sit inside of the network and data link layers previously discussed in this section.

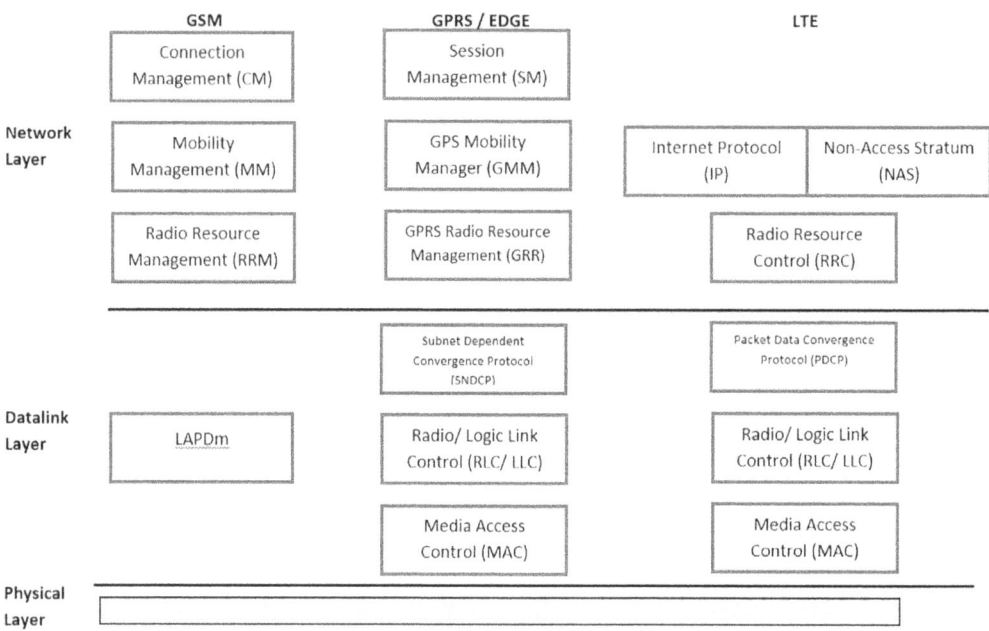

Figure 18 - GSM network layers

Information Elements

Layer 3 messages consist of at least one octet. These messages include two parts, an imperative and non-imperative part. Both of these parts comprise information elements (IEs), which in turn comprise a half octet or more. IEs have the following components:

- **Information Element Identifier (IEI)** – Consisting of a half octet or one octet
- **A Length Indicator (LI)** – Consisting of one octet, this component contains the number of octets of the IE occurring after the LI component.
- **A Value Part (VP)** – Consisting of a minimum of half an octet. This may be further structured into fields.

Standard Information elements will have one of the formats detailed in Table 14 - Information element breakdown:

Format	Meaning	IEI Present	LI Present	Value Part Present
T	Type Only	Yes	No	No
V	Value Only	No	No	Yes
TV	Type and Value	Yes	No	Yes
LV	Length and Value	No	Yes	Yes
TLV	Type, Length, and Value	Yes	Yes	Yes

Table 14 - Information element breakdown

Further to this, there are five categories of standard information elements defined as:

- **Type One** – An information element of format V or TV with a value part of half an octet.
- **Type Two** – An information element of format T with a value part of 0 octets.
- **Type Three** – An information element of format V or TV with a value part with a fixed length of at least one octet.
- **Type Four** – An information element of format TLV or LV with a value part of zero, one, or more octets.
- **Type Five** – An information element of format V with a value part of 0, one, or more octets.

Reverse Engineering A Modern Baseband

As specified earlier in this chapter, there are many different baseband implementations that all come with their own quirks and structures. This section will walk through a method for reverse engineering and identifying vulnerabilities in modern baseband implementations, as shown in Figure 19 - Baseband vulnerability analysis breakdown.

As part of this method, each section will be discussed at a high level, and where examples are required, the Shannon baseband implementation will be used.

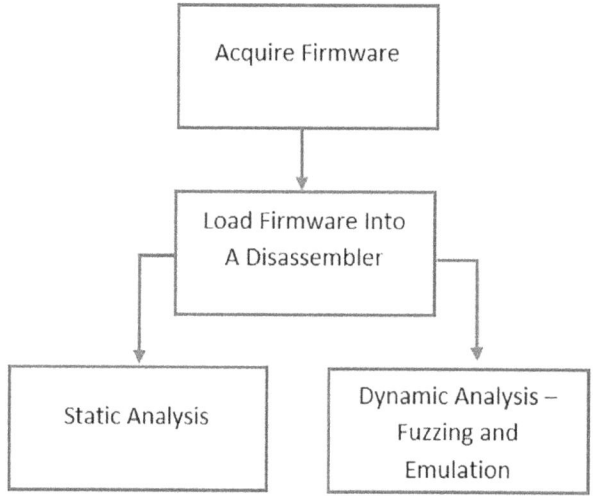

Figure 19 - Baseband vulnerability analysis breakdown

Acquire Firmware

There are several ways to acquire the firmware for a given baseband implementation. These are discussed at a high level below:

- **Intercepting a device's update process** – In most cases, baseband firmware is updated over the air where the entire firmware (rather than just an update) may be sent to the device. In these cases, it is possible to intercept this firmware for loading into a disassembler. On newer devices, it is common to find that this firmware is encrypted.
- **Locating previously acquired firmware from other researcher** – Depending on their research, some researchers and hobbyists upload the firmware they have acquired to online platforms and repositories.
- **Acquiring the firmware from the manufacturer** – Some manufacturers release their baseband firmware as open-source or have downloads to the firmware binaries. This is less common for newer baseband implementations.
- **Retrieve firmware from device filesystem** – On some rooted Android devices, the baseband firmware can be retrieved from the radio partition.

- **Retrieve firmware from modem memory** – In some cases, it's possible to retrieve the baseband firmware from the modem memory or from crash dumps.

Example:

When looking at the Shannon baseband, we can look at how we could acquire the firmware for a device. Depending on the model and version, there are a few options. If the version is available online via `https://www.sammobile.com/firmwares/` or `https://github.com/grant-h/ShannonFirmware`, we may just want to download the modem.bin file from there. Otherwise, we can either acquire the `modem.bin` file from the radio partition or from a ramdump of the modem (common if root isn't available on the device). In addition to this, it is possible on some Samsung devices to use the dialer and call *#9090# or *#9900# to access `Service Mode` and from the `RAMDUMP` dialogue to run `RUN FORCED CP CRASH DUMP` and to have `DEBUG LEVEL ENABLED HIGH`.[8] [9] [10] This allows for a crash dump where the modem memory can be read.

Load Firmware Into a Disassembler

Once you have acquired the baseband firmware, you will need to load it into a disassembler/ decompiler to start your analysis. As most firmware is of a proprietary format, does not include symbols, or (if it was acquired via a ram dump) may not be in a continuous layout, effort needs to be spent in loading it into a readable form. This may involve identifying the symbol table in the firmware and casting it to a struct.

If the symbol table can't be located (or one hasn't been compiled into the binary), labels (or partial labels) can be created by checking if the function:

- Calls known APIs
- Contains a directory structure
- Contains a file name
- Contains a string or fuzzy string

---

[8] https://github.com/Comsecuris/shannonRE

[9] https://hardwear.io/netherlands-2020/presentation/samsung-baseband-hardwear-io-nl-2020.pdf

[10] https://github.com/grant-h/ShannonBaseband

Example:

For example, when looking at Shannon, we can use the techniques mentioned in the previous section to acquire a `modem.bin` file. For the purposes of this example, they have been retrieved from the `https://github.com/grant-h/ShannonFirmware` repository. After this, we can load the binary into a disassembler (i.e., Ghidra or IDA) and begin the automated analysis of the binary. Once this has been completed, we can see that the binary has loaded successfully, and some functions have been identified. However, these functions remain nameless.

Several scripts have been developed by other researchers for the purpose of refactoring function names inside of the Shannon binary - `https://github.com/optitree/baseband-balong-firmware-markup/blob/master/markup-ida.py` and `https://github.com/grant-h/ShannonBaseband/blob/master/reversing/ghidra/scripts/ShannonRename.py`.

Static Analysis of Baseband Firmware

As discussed previously in this book, static analysis incorporates reviewing the source, disassembled, or decompiled code for security issues or information. When it comes to modern baseband implementations we would want to focus on the following:

- **Identification of RTOS tasks** – As most modern baseband implementations are built on top of an RTOS, the RTOS tasks function as entry points to the protocols being used.
- **Identification of over the air (OTA) reachable functions** – Such as the radio interface or other OTA functions.
- **Memory corruption vulnerabilities** – One of the most common types of vulnerabilities found in modern basebands is memory corruption bugs. These can be found where memory is directly accessed, where a memcpy is insecurely used, or where a secure memcpy has a controllable destination and source length.

Example:

In Shannon, RTOS task entry points are defined as `TaskEntry_<Protocol name>`. This being the case, if our firmware loading scripts have worked successfully, we should be able to search for all functions matching the `TaskEntry_` string to identify all our task entry points. If the loading scripts have not worked successfully, then there are a few options to identify these task entry points—either by identifying these entry points via strings in the binary or by finding functions relating to protocols (i.e., SMS, LTE, etc.) and then tracing the references back to their entry point.

Dynamic Analysis – Fuzzing and Emulation

When performing a more complex analysis of modern baseband implementations, it may be pertinent to perform fuzzing or emulation of the baseband setup. No public, out of the box tools exist for this, and so there are currently two recommended approaches, these being:

- **Targeted Emulation** – Targeted emulation is where emulation and fuzzing are performed on a specific aspect of the baseband. For example, a specific entry point or set of functions.
- **Full System Emulation** – As the name suggests, full system emulation is where the entire baseband system (or at least a large portion) is emulated.

Example:

Carrying on with the Shannon example, the Unicorn library from AFL++ can be used (or other targeted emulation frameworks, such as Ghidra's built in PCode emulation) to emulate and fuzz a specific task entry point. Unlike full system emulation, targeted emulation is significantly less involved, and Unicorn can be configured easily. However, it will provide less realistic and more varied results.

CHAPTER SEVEN

PUTTING IT TO THE TEST

This book's main purpose is to be a day-to-day reference guide for security researchers looking for a quick answer or fix. While that's the case, for many new researchers, it's also important to have a structured way of trialing out these techniques before getting your hands dirty for real. This chapter breaks down several challenges based on sections throughout the book that can be used as a structure to practice, experiment with, and develop your skills with the aforementioned technologies and principles.

What this section is

- A series of challenge templates that can be used to enhance or develop your expertise in the technologies in previous chapters.

What this section is not

- A guided walkthrough of the technologies (see the previous chapters).

Tools used throughout this section

- See respective chapters for related required tooling.

Challenge One | Keys To The Kingdom

INTRO TO DEVELOPMENT AND REVERSE ENGINEERING CHALLENGE

DURATION: 8 HOURS

REFERENCE: CHAPTER TWO

Learning outcomes

- A basic understanding of C development and the C programming language useful for reverse engineering.
- An introductory knowledge of reverse engineering techniques and tooling.

Summary

This challenge sets the groundwork for a series of hands-on training covering core principles and techniques required in the vulnerability research and reverse engineering field—including scripting and development, reverse engineering, and vulnerability research skills. The first half of this pathway will see you create a simple password manager in C and incorporate a vulnerability into its design. After this, you'll reverse engineer and either manually exploit the vulnerability or create a fuzzer and test harness to discover the vulnerability.

Steps

1. Develop a CLI Password manager in C with the following key features:
   a. Stores encoded passwords
   b. Runs as root
   c. Takes a parameter master password
   d. Has the ability to add new passwords to the manager

2. Taking the password manager, incorporate a simple vulnerability that can be reached via the parameter input master password or a similar entry point
   a. String injection attacks, such as SQLi, XSS, CSRF, system() calls
   b. Format string bugs
   c. Buffer overflows
   d. Use-after-free
   e. Null pointer dereference
   f. Use of uninitialized variables
   g. Type confusion
   h. Race conditions
   i. Heap corruption
3. Compile the password manager (make sure to exclude mechanisms such as ASLR) and open it in a disassembler (such as IDA or Ghidra). Then look for the following:
   a. Entry points
   b. Complex functions
   c. Libraries and imports
   d. Is the program obfuscated?
4. Either manually exploit the vulnerability to cause a crash or develop a fuzzer and test harness.

Challenge Two | Build It, And They Will Come

INTRO TO DEVELOPMENT, NETWORKING, AND REVERSE ENGINEERING CHALLENGE

DURATION: 8 HOURS

REFERENCE: CHAPTER TWO

Learning outcomes

- A basic understanding of C development and the C programming language useful for reverse engineering.
- An understanding of networking techniques and principles put into practice.
- An introductory knowledge of reverse engineering techniques and tooling.

Summary

This challenge builds on previous hands-on training, covering core principles and techniques required in the vulnerability research and reverse engineering field. The first half of this challenge will see you create a chat server and client in Python, Java, and C and incorporate a vulnerability into its design. After this, you'll take your chat server, reverse engineer it, and manually exploit the vulnerability and create a fuzzer and test harness to discover one.

Steps

1. Develop a chat server (that communicates with a client) in Python utilizing sockets. The chat server should be able to send messages, save messages, have an online status, and have the ability for new users to be registered.
2. Develop two additional clients for the chat server. One client should be written for Android and the other written in C or C++.

3. Incorporate a vulnerability into each client (C and Java) to be accessible over the air or via user input.
   - String injection attacks, such as SQLi, XSS, CSRF, system() calls
   - Format string bugs
   - Buffer overflows
   - Use-after-free
   - Null pointer dereference
   - Use of uninitialized variables
   - Type confusion
   - Race conditions
   - Heap corruption
4. Reverse engineer your clients and identify the following: Entry points, Complex functions, Libraries and imports, and obfuscation. Manually identify and exploit the vulnerability in their Python and Android clients.
5. Using AFL Unicorn in the AFL++ package, develop a fuzzer and harness for the C client. You may need to develop multiple harnesses, including OTA (Over the air) inputs and local user inputs.

Challenge Three | Droid's Clues

INTRO TO ANDROID DEVELOPMENT AND ANDROID REVERSE ENGINEERING

DURATION: 8 HOURS

REFERENCE: CHAPTER FIVE

Learning outcomes

- Android application development skills and Java knowledge—useful for reverse engineering Java applications
- Android application reverse engineering skills

Summary

This challenge sees you create a simple Android application in Java and then reverse engineer that application with a suite of tools. The first half of this challenge should involve you developing a simple application in Java. Some examples can be seen below:

- A simple tracker to count the water you've drunk in a day.
- A date and time application.
- An application that performs a simple HTTP web request.
- A simple calculator.
- A note taking application.

For the second half of this challenge, you should compile your application (consider compiling it as a release build with obfuscation enabled) and use the APK tool and Jad-x GUI on the APK. Seek to identify the following:

- Application permissions – in the manifest file, what permissions are requested.

- Application entry point – where does the application start execution (defined in the manifest)?
- Application functionality – you developed this application, so this phase should be easy. Identify the main purpose of the application and how it is used.

Steps

1. Develop a simple Android application and compile it as a release build.
2. Take the compiled APK and open it up in APK Tool and JAD-X GUI (or similar tools).
   a. You may wish to install the APK onto a device and then extract it off the device as practice.
3. Identify the key functionality of the application using reverse engineering techniques.

Challenge Four | Thinking With Hooks

INTRO TO ANDROID DEVELOPMENT AND HOOKING WITH FRIDA

DURATION: 8 HOURS

REFERENCE: CHAPTER FOUR

Learning outcomes

- Android application development skills and Java knowledge—useful for reverse engineering Java applications.
- Frida application hooking skills.
- Android application reverse engineering skills.

Summary

This challenge sees you create a simple Android application, deploy that application onto an Android device, and then (using Frida) hook that application to achieve hidden functionality. For the first half of this challenge, you should create a simple Android application. This application should be simple in design, focusing on a few key features; some examples can be seen below:

- A simple note-taking application
- A quote of the day application
- A simple password manager
- An Android file explorer

Irrespective of the application type you choose, you should also develop a hidden feature in the application. This hidden feature can be as simple as displaying a Toast notification popup on the screen when a function is called. It is important to note that if this function is not being called by the program normally, then ensure that compilation optimization is disabled and that you are building the debug application—this will ensure that the function isn't removed as part of compile-time optimization.

The second half of this challenge should involve taking the application and installing it onto an emulator or device. Then extract the APK from the device and decompile it to identify the hidden function. After this, either patch the application with Frida or install Frida onto the device (requires root) and call the secret function using dynamic instrumentation.

Steps

1. Develop a simple Android application in Java. Don't spend more than half of your time on this.
2. Incorporate a hidden function into the application where a Toast notification is displayed on the screen when called.
3. Compile the application and run it on a device.
4. Extract the APK from the device and disassemble it (i.e., with Jadx-gui)
5. Identify the hidden function, and after installing Frida on a rooted device or patching the application with Frida, attempt to call the hidden function to trigger the toast notification.

Challenge Five | All Your Basebands

INTRO TO THE SHANNON BASEBAND AND BASEBAND REVERSE ENGINEERING

DURATION: 8 HOURS

REFERENCE: CHAPTER SIX

Learning outcomes

- An understanding of how the Shannon Baseband is architected
- An introductory look at how to reverse engineer basebands
- A stronger understanding of how basebands operate

Summary

This challenge takes a hands-off approach to guiding you through better understanding baseband architectures by acquiring the firmware and then reverse engineering a version of the Shannon baseband. For this challenge, you will need to acquire a copy of the Shannon firmware (see above on page 76, Acquire Firmware). Once acquired, you will need to load the firmware into a disassembler such as Ghidra or IDA (as explained on pages 77 and 78). After this stage, you may wish to continue your learning and may wish to develop a simple fuzzing harness for the firmware (see page 79 for more information on this).

Steps

1. Acquire a copy of the Shannon firmware (any version will be sufficient)
2. Load the firmware into a disassembler (i.e., Ghidra or IDA)
3. Identify key aspects of the application, such as:
   a. Known protocols (i.e., from strings)

       b.   RTOS task entry points

       c.   The radio interface

4.   You may wish to continue with this challenge further and develop a targeted fuzzing harness for the firmware using Unicorn, a part of AFL++.

CHAPTER EIGHT

CLOSING THOUGHTS

This book has discussed an array of offensive security techniques related to the Android and iOS operating systems and highlights wider technologies in the field of mobile offensive security—including baseband. The purpose of this book has been to serve as a reference guide and introduction to the core principles and techniques used in mobile offensive security.

This book is the product and evolution of my work in the mobile offensive security space and came from developing a reference guide that I used in my day-to-day activities.

While this book serves as an easy to pick up reference guide for mobile offensive security techniques, if you are looking to take your knowledge of the area further, then I strongly suggest reviewing the challenges in the previous chapter (from page 81) and building on them as well as developing your own projects and ideas.

2021 has been a long and hard year for many, and I would like to close this book off by thanking everyone who has supported me over the past few years, especially my family, friends, and partner. I'd also like to thank JD, an old manager of mine, who inspired me to write my first book, without which I wouldn't be here writing my second. In addition to this, after several years of working with the team at Interrupt Labs, many of the principles and methods I've learnt from them over the years have made their way into this book—thank you for your support and knowledge.

Other Resources

There are a plethora of other amazing resources out there to support your knowledge in mobile offensive security; a selection of these has been included here:

- **Azeria Labs** – ARM tutorials |
  `https://azeria-labs.com/writing-arm-assembly-part-1`
- **Maddie Stone** – Android reverse engineering tutorials |
  `https://www.ragingrock.com/AndroidAppRE/`
- **Jonathan Levin** – Android Internals: A Confectioner's
  Cookbook `http://newandroidbook.com/`

More From The Author

For more information and resources from me, the author of this book, James Stevenson, please visit my website at https://www.JamesStevenson.me/.

If you enjoyed this book, you might also be interested in my previous writing, *Android Software Internals Quick Reference: A Field Manual and Security Reference Guide to Java-based Android Components*, available on most book websites[11].

I've also put together a course on *Learning Reverse Engineering With Android Games* if you'd like to put the lessons learnt in this book to further test[12].

---

[11] https://amzn.to/3JBySCA

[12] https://www.udemy.com/course/learn-reverse-engineering-through-android-games/?referralCode=CBA2
4934A92B1E58B76C

TABLE OF FIGURES

INDEX